Praise for *Out F*

"Deborah walks you through the anxiety, terror, and often debilitating fear of public speaking, while handing you the keys to break free and confidently share your authentic voice in a meaningful and memorable way! With practice, *Out Front* might even make speaking in public actually fun!"

—Actress Demi Moore

"Deborah debunks public speaking myths and will have you wondering how she got into your head. You won't be able to make excuses any longer."

—Eden Gillott Bowe, President, Gillott Communications LLC

"Every time I see Deborah or read this book, I learn more to help me become a better speaker. I gain confidence to prepare, practice, and present more powerful presentations."

—Lauren O'Donnell, Global General Manager and Vice President, life sciences industry, IBM

"Through my work with Deborah I have completely transformed as a public speaker. I've stopped apologizing—in speech, in body language, in cues—for stating my position and I now have a tool kit to achieve my goals."

—Julie Cordua, CEO, Thorn: Digital Defenders of Children

"At some point, I forgot what I was reading because it was so personal and conversational. *Out Front* has changed me. Reading this book convinced me that I didn't need to be PERFECT. I hope this book inspires many women who are experiencing the same anxiety I did."

—Ellen Lee, Human Resources Manager, Lotte Advanced Materials

"After reading *Out Front* I realized that I should embrace my individuality and utilize it as a competitive advantage."

—Debra Gentz, Vice President, Bank of the West

"Deborah, the tiny woman who fills up every room she enters, centers and calms the reader by sharing her power tools that give us both the courage and confidence to find our voice within and to deliver our messages with the impact that makes them stick."

—DeeDee DeMan, Chairman and CEO, Bench International

"As *Out Front* says, if we are to become successful, we need to constantly go outside our comfort zone. As I transitioned into a new leadership role at a multibillion-dollar organization, Deborah's book was spot on! I used some of the pointers when meeting my new colleagues with an air of confidence that was critical in a male-dominated industry."

—Caryn Siebert, Vice President of Claims, Knight Insurance Group (a Hankey Group company)

"Deborah's book changed the way I think about, prepare, and deliver presentations and speeches. *Out Front* gave me the confidence and courage to just be me and tell my story, and I believe this book will empower many women to go out front and do the same."

—Julie Fleshman, President and CEO, Pancreatic Cancer Action Network

"*Out Front* is the definitive guide for how women can 'lean in,' be memorable, and be graciously and gracefully formidable without becoming the 'B' word."

—Dr. Mark Goulston, Author of *Just Listen: Discover the Secret to Getting Through to Absolutely Anyone*, Co-host of *It's Your Health* on NPR, and Co-founder, Heartfelt Leadership

"Are you looking to own the room like Beyoncé? Go for it with *Out Front*! This is a must-read for the businesswoman on her path to brilliant success on and off the speaking stage."

—Lolita Taub, Vice President of Sales, Glassbreakers, Millennial Tech Intrapreneur and Social Entrepreneur

"If you're ready to stop abdicating to the boys being consistently 'out front,' you hold in your hand the book that will give you new insights and tools to exponentially increase confidence in speaking. If you're ready to take your career to the next level, this is a must-read."

—Elizabeth Bishop, Executive Senior Vice President, Heffernan Insurance

"As someone who loves to speak in public, but still gets anxious, reading this book is like a private coaching session with Deborah. I appreciate the heartfelt support she gives her readers and the encouragement to overcome their fear."

—Cheryl Bame, Principal of Bame Public Relations

"Every woman executive who might feel uncomfortable being 'out front' will gain confidence, effectiveness, and perhaps for the first time, actually enjoy speaking before audiences—as I now do, thanks to the invaluable counsel Deborah gives in *Out Front*."

—Betsy Berkhemer-Credaire, Author of *The Board Game: How Smart Women Become Corporate Directors* and Co-owner of Berkhemer Clayton Retained Executive Search

"*Out Front* changed my entire perspective about public speaking. It went from something I used to dread to something I get paid to do! I am buying copies for all my employees—women and men—because I want to see them go through the same transformation I did."

—Liz Davidson, CEO of Financial Finesse and Author of *What Your Financial Advisor Isn't Telling You: The 10 Essential Truths You Need to Know About Your Money*

"If you read only one book about speaking, this must be the book. It's overflowing with practical advice from how to craft your talk to what to do in the ten minutes before you step in front of the audience."

—Lanie Denslow, Author of *World Wise: What to Know Before You Go*

"This book is not only for emerging women professionals, but for those of us with twenty years' experience in front of an audience. Deborah's sage voice is in my head every time I create a presentation or update tested material. I may just wallpaper my office with the pages of *Out Front*."

—Karen L. Cates, Ph.D., Executive Coach, Leadership Development Consultant, and Adjunct Professor of Executive Education at the Kellogg School of Management at Northwestern University

"*Out Front* is a call to professional women to speak authentically and powerfully. Deborah Shames speaks compelling truths that support us in overcoming the obstacles that block us from engaging our audiences."

—Sharon Rich, Founder and CEO, thinkbusinessgrowth powered by IMPAQ

"Filled with illuminating tips, tools, and real-life examples, *Out Front* by Deborah Shames is an exceptional guide for any woman desiring to be a more engaging and powerful presenter."

—Dr. Lonnie Barbach, Author of *For Yourself: The Fulfillment of Female Sexuality* and other books

"*Out Front* is an experiential guide to what all professional women need to know about public speaking."

—Harriet Welch, Partner, law firm of Squire Patton Boggs

"This book is much more than how women can become engaging, memorable, and fearless speakers—it's about how women can reach inside themselves and bring out their authentic voice to any job or situation."

—Carla Hatley, Producer, Fratelli Bologna

"Truly life changing, inspiring, and honest. I was cheering at the end for myself and every other little girl who shuffled to the edge and jumped—all because you believed and showed us how, Deborah!"

—Margaret Bayston, CEO and President, Laura's House

"Deborah clearly understands the issues many professionals face, both internally and externally. She strikes a balance between sharing personal experiences and weaving in other leaders' relevant insights and quotes. This is a must-read if you speak publicly, whether to a large group or to a few peers."

—Ellen Anreder, President and CEO, Bleiweiss Communications Inc.

"Deborah offers not only her personal support and knowledge of the path but all the practical tools and techniques she honed along the way. Read this book and Deborah will be your human GPS and guide you to your place *Out Front!*"

—Barbara McMahon, Executive Coach, Trainer, and Author

"It's fabulous. Deborah addressed the issues confronting speakers—from anxiety to storytelling. Once you read *Out Front*, you don't need to read any other book on public speaking. Go, Deborah."

—Ada Deer, Former Assistant Secretary of Indian affairs, U.S. Department of Interior

Out Front

Shames, Deborah, 1950-
Out front : how women
can become engaging, mem
[2017]
33305238638682
ca   04/28/17

Out Front

HOW WOMEN CAN BECOME ENGAGING, MEMORABLE, AND FEARLESS SPEAKERS

Deborah Shames

BENBELLA

BenBella Books, Inc.
Dallas, TX

Copyright © 2017 by Eloqui: Presentation and Communication Training

All rights reserved. No part of this book may be used or reproduced in any manner whatsoever without written permission except in the case of brief quotations embodied in critical articles or reviews.

This material has been written and published for educational purposes to enhance one's knowledge about public speaking and to improve abilities in this area. The content of the book is the sole expression and opinion of the author and does not necessarily reflect the views of the publisher.

Throughout this book, stories and examples of typical client experiences are used to illustrate and allow the reader to better understand the techniques and processes described. While these anecdotes about clients are based on real experiences, client names and other characteristics have been changed to protect individuals' privacy.

BenBella Books, Inc.
10440 N. Central Expressway, Suite 800
Dallas, Texas 75231
www.benbellabooks.com
Send feedback to feedback@benbellabooks.com

Printed in the United States of America
10 9 8 7 6 5 4 3 2 1

Library of Congress Cataloging-in-Publication Data
Names: Shames, Deborah, 1950- author.
Title: Out front : how women can become engaging, memorable, and fearless
    speakers / by Deborah Shames.
Description: Dallas, TX : BenBella Books, Inc., 2017. | Includes
    bibliographical references and index.
Identifiers: LCCN 2016025286 (print) | LCCN 2016043689 (ebook) | ISBN
    9781941631676 (trade paper : alk. paper) | ISBN 9781941631683 (electronic)
Subjects: LCSH: Public speaking for women.
Classification: LCC PN4192.W65 S54 2017 (print) | LCC PN4192.W65 (ebook) |
    DDC 808.5/1082—dc23
LC record available at https://lccn.loc.gov/2016025286

Editing by Amy Debra Feldman
Copyediting by Brian J. Buchanan
Text design and composition by Aaron Edmiston
Proofreading by Lisa Story and Cape Cod
    Compositors, Inc.
Front cover design by Baker Brand
    Communications
Full cover design by Sarah Dombrowsky
Cover photo by Yee-Ping Cho, featuring model
    Lauren Haas, Haas Holistic
Printed by Lake Book Manufacturing

Distributed by Perseus Distribution
www.perseusdistribution.com

To place orders through Perseus Distribution:
Tel: (800) 343-4499
Fax: (800) 351-5073
E-mail: orderentry@perseusbooks.com

Special discounts for bulk sales (minimum of 25 copies) are available.
Please contact Aida Herrera at aida@benbellabooks.com.

To Luciana Perri, one of the bravest women I've ever met, who overcame extreme stage fright to become a shining example for others. Even in her personal life, Lu pushed her limits. She was diving on a shipwreck off the coast of Canada when we lost her far too soon.

CONTENTS

Introduction   xiii

1   Inspirational and Powerful Female Icons   1
2   Exorcise the Demons: Dispelling Myths about Public Speaking   9
3   Afraid to Misspeak: Perfection Is a Bitch   37
4   What Sets Us Apart: Playing to Our Strengths   51
5   Read Your Audience: The Eloqui Communication Index   63
6   The Value of Using Strong Technique   75
7   Engage the Audience from Start to Finish   95
8   Move with Purpose   105
9   Technology—Friend or Foe?   111
10 Serve and Volley: Communication as a Contact Sport   117
11 Perception Is Reality: Reprogramming Our Mind-Set   139
12 Manage Anxiety and Deliver like a Pro   149
13 Your Formula for Success: One Step at a Time   167

Acknowledgments   175
Appendix: Trusted Advisor Template©   177
Glossary   179
Endnotes   183
About the Author   191

INTRODUCTION

*"It's a sad day when you find out that it's not accident or time or fortune,
but just yourself that kept things from you."*
—Lillian Hellman

I confess. To this day, I experience anxiety before delivering a keynote or leading my business group. I have trouble quieting my mind and sleeping the night before. I imagine everything that could go wrong, and question whether I've prepared enough.

This may not sound like a surprising admission, since 74 percent of the US population surveyed in 2013 shares a fear of public speaking.[1] What's unusual is that I speak regularly to large audiences around the United States—despite having this fear. I even formed a company called Eloqui, with my partner, David Booth, to train and coach professionals to be effective presenters and communicators.

Over time, I've learned to manage my anxiety and turn it into an engine that propels me forward. As I tell my clients, *some* anxiety is a good thing. It says your presentation is important. Anxiety means your brain is firing on all cylinders. And you're in the moment, focused on the task at hand. The trick is never to let your doubts stop you from speaking out.

The trick is never to let your doubts stop you from speaking out.

Before founding Eloqui, I was a film and television director. For more than fifteen years I worked behind the scenes, directing actors and business executives to deliver their strongest performances. During that period, I produced and/or directed more than sixty award-winning films and videos.

But common wisdom says you teach what you most need to know, and that applied to me. I was certain that whenever I spoke in public, the audience sat silently in judgment—as if my own internal critic weren't harsh enough.

The flip side was that I *knew* speaking engagements would heighten my credibility as a director and accelerate the growth of my production company. Even then, I realized that when you address an audience, you're seen as the go-to person in your industry—whether you're a paid speaker or volunteer. At the time, I'd rather have had a root canal than voluntarily address a business group, be interviewed by the press, or speak at a conference where I was presented as an expert.

Naturally, because of my fear of public speaking, or glossophobia (in Greek, *glosso* means tongue; *phobos* means fear), I avoided most speaking opportunities. If, in a moment of weakness, I'd agreed to give a talk, sheer terror would set in immediately. I'd wake up every morning agonizing over the upcoming presentation and obsess about creative ways to cancel. This mental tug of war went on for weeks before the actual engagement.

By the time I stood up to address the audience, my fear of failure had become a self-fulfilling prophecy. The ability to think on my feet vanished. My quavering voice rose an octave, and I felt like I was having an out-of-body experience. Afraid of making a fool of myself by leaving something out, I read my neatly typed, double-spaced copy word for word. Needless to say, I wasn't the most engaging speaker. If I could make it through the ordeal without passing out, I'd consider the experience a success.

I apologize to anyone who sat through my generic speeches back in the pre-Eloqui days. Like most audiences, you were polite and encouraging. You undoubtedly attended my talk because you hoped you would come away with a new insight or fresh perspective. But because I followed a standard template, most likely you were bored and could predict what I'd say next.

It finally occurred to me that most people aren't innately good at public speaking. The solution was right in front of me. I'd spent fifteen years directing performers to reach inside for emotional realism and sincerity. I needed to take my own advice.

Becoming an engaging speaker requires skill, courage, and an unwavering commitment to connect with an audience. This means incorporating your own perspective and personality into presentations. Because of my fear of making a mistake, I did the opposite. Like so many women speakers, I excised every unique element that would have made me memorable. No wonder my stage presence didn't exude confidence and my presentations rarely seemed genuine.

Then something clicked. I remember it like it was yesterday, but years ago David and I were contracted to deliver a two-hour keynote speech titled, "What Actors Can Teach Litigators." The room was packed with 400 attorneys from a prestigious national firm. We were center stage at the Beverly Hilton, where the Golden Globe and Emmy Awards have been telecast. Before that day, walking into that huge ballroom—even empty—would have paralyzed me.

There was also the added pressure of addressing attorneys. I knew the audience had high expectations and would question whether our talk was worth giving up their valuable billable hours. We were promoted as experts, and a lot was riding on that designation. Just thinking about it made my heart pound. I was afraid my internal critic would strangle any rational thought, and the presentation would be a disaster.

I decided that it was within me to change my approach, and engineer the perception I chose. With my determination and David's encouragement, we adopted a new method of preparation. Instead of writing a script, we drafted an outline. Before the talk, we interviewed an attorney from the firm to determine what would be most valuable to our audience. We brainstormed anecdotes and decided which of us would lead each section. Then we rehearsed, without attempting to be perfect or investing our full energy. The night before the big day, I took a hot bath and slept seven blissful hours.

I'd be lying if I said I didn't still obsess over the talk. It was like a mosquito buzzing around my ears, but this time the pest didn't bite. Instead of focusing on the critic in my head, I imagined our success and employed performer techniques, including *sense memory*, to manage the anxiety (see chapter twelve, "Manage Anxiety and Deliver like a Pro," for more on sense memory).

The morning of the presentation we arrived early to check out the space. Before entering the room, I thought about what I wanted to achieve. Just before our introduction, I did a breathing exercise to bring my heart rate back to normal. During the keynote, our outline stayed on the lectern. I was able to cover the entire stage, walking over casually to check my notes only when necessary. I made eye contact with the audience, embellished an anecdote or two, and on occasion injected personal comments that were well received.

About five minutes in, I began to have a good time. The positive response from the audience energized me. Their support gave me confidence. I discovered what actors mean when they say they *owned the room* during a great performance. It was thrilling—similar to the time I jumped out of an airplane and looked up to see the beautiful red, yellow, and blue colors of my parachute open against the sky!

I discovered what actors mean when they say they *owned the room* during a great performance.

Often speakers (like the old me) strive to educate an audience to prove their expertise or deliver in a manner they believe is expected of them. This takes an enormous amount of preparation, ramps up anxiety, and rarely achieves one's intention. It's much more powerful and effective to persuade an audience. Better yet, it takes the focus off the speaker and puts it where it belongs, squarely on the audience.

David spent many years as a professional actor. When I combined his knowledge with my experience directing actors, I realized I had the secret sauce. Great performers are masters of emotional persuasion. They understand Intention, the complexities of Roles, how to manage anxiety, tell a great story, move in a space, and turn any script into a gripping narrative.

Every professional actor knows that audiences connect with a performer who's perceived as authentic and committed to the character she's playing. Similarly in business, speakers who reveal something meaningful about themselves (or their take on a subject) can expect a high likability quotient. Audiences trust and respond to a speaker who provides a window into her thinking, even if they don't agree with her.

As a former director, I know the value of practical techniques. It's nearly impossible to follow the advice to "be confident," "be yourself," or "give more emotionally." That's why *Out Front* is balanced between identifying women's challenges in communicating and providing an operating manual on how to overcome them.

But technique is only part of the equation. Learning to identify and express your core differences, strengths, and authenticity isn't easy. George Burns said it best: "Acting is all about honesty. If you can fake that, you've got it made." The same goes for speaking in public, making a presentation, or communicating with others.

In *Out Front* I share the performance techniques that David and I have translated for business professionals. The anecdotes about clients throughout the book are based on real experiences, but client names and other characteristics have been changed to protect their privacy.

This book focuses on the strengths and challenges facing women speakers because that's what I know best. However, the techniques presented here are practical, field-tested, and proven. When these are put into practice, women *and* men can become engaging, memorable, and fearless speakers.

1

INSPIRATIONAL AND POWERFUL FEMALE ICONS

There have always been women who had the moxie to stand up and speak out. Today, many women are making unique contributions in politics, entertainment, and business.

As a college student, I embraced an alternative lifestyle. Before my junior year, I changed majors from education to anthropology and transferred from Northern Illinois University to the University of Wisconsin–Madison. It was the 1960s, and the pass/fail grading system at UW allowed me time to protest the Vietnam War and participate in campus politics. Even my decision to study cultural anthropology was about making a contribution to the world rather than making money. Thank goodness my parents gave me a long leash, especially when they very much wanted me to graduate, get a job, and become financially self-sufficient. But I believed that going corporate, owning property, or driving a gas-guzzling car was being co-opted by the establishment and just plain wrong. Ah, college and the naiveté of youth.

This narrow perspective severely limited my career choices. But when you're twenty-one and on your own for the first time, anything and everything seems possible. And I was fortunate to have powerful female icons who served as role models, both personally and for women worldwide.

In 1972, Gloria Steinem co-founded *Ms. Magazine* and took a stand on women venturing out on their own. She popularized the phrase, "A woman needs a man like a fish needs a bicycle," which resonated with me.[2]

I was equally impressed with the chutzpah of authors such as Germaine Greer, who wrote *The Female Eunuch* and railed against the conservatism of the day. Greer was described as an "impulsive, fatally naive diva of feminism who made the world a better place in spite of herself."[3] Or Erica Jong, author of *Fear of Flying*, who celebrated women's newfound sexual freedom. As you'll read later, I picked up her banner with the genre of films I produced. Now Jong's book *Fear of Dying* completes the arc of time.[4] Aging has a way of giving us perspective on the totality of our lives.

In politics, I was moved by the eloquence of Congresswoman Barbara Jordan, the first black woman to serve in the United States House of Representatives. Two of Jordan's talks are included in *American Rhetoric*'s list of the 100 greatest speeches of all time.[5] At the 1976 Democratic National Convention, Jordan delivered a moving and powerful call to action. Hard to believe it was forty years ago. Following is an excerpt: "And now—now we must look to the future. Let us heed the voice of the people and recognize their common sense. If we do not, we not only blaspheme our political heritage, we ignore the common ties that bind all Americans. Many fear the future. Many are distrustful of their leaders, and believe that their voices are never heard. Many seek only to satisfy their private work—wants; to satisfy their private interests. But this is the great danger America faces—that we will cease to be one nation and become instead a collection of interest groups: city against suburb, region against region, individual against individual; each seeking to satisfy private wants. If that happens, who then will speak for America? Who then will speak for the common good?"[6]

I also admired the outspoken U.S. Representative Bella Abzug, who wore her trademark floppy hat on the House floor to avoid being mistaken for a congressional assistant who might be asked to fetch coffee. In her words: "When I first became a lawyer, only 2 percent of the bar was women. People would always think I was a secretary. In those days, professional women in the business world wore hats. So I started wearing hats."[7] Abzug provided many quotable statements, but this one says it all: "We are bringing women into politics to change the nature of politics, to change the vision, to change the institutions. Women are not wedded to the policies of the past. We didn't craft them. They didn't let us."[8]

At the opposite end of the spectrum was the soft-spoken yet effective Patricia Schroeder. In a sea of male congressional representatives, Schroeder was the first female representative elected from Colorado, as well as the first woman to serve on the male-dominated House Armed Services Committee.[9] I'll bet she wasn't popular for publicly stating that "When men talk about defense, they always claim to be protecting women and children, but they never ask the women and children what they think."[10] Always the strategist, Schroeder realized that a light touch would allow her words to carry more weight. For example, "When people ask me why I am running as a woman, I always answer, what choice do I have?"[11]

There were also role models in my personal life. For these specific individuals, I will refer to them by their first names because they became my friends. While studying at the University of Wisconsin, I was introduced to Ada Deer, an advocate for indigenous peoples. Among her many accomplishments, Ada served as chairwoman of the Menominee Restoration Committee (the interim tribal government). Later, appointed by President Bill Clinton, she was the first woman to serve as assistant secretary of Indian Affairs in the Department of the Interior.[12] In her confirmation hearing, she said she wanted the Bureau of Indian Affairs to be a full partner in fulfilling the Indian agenda developed in Indian country. "The best way we can do this is for the tribes to decide what needs to be done and for the tribes to do it on their own terms, with our enthusiastic support."[13] Here again, a female leader advocated for self-determination.

Shortly after graduating college in the early 1970s, I volunteered to work with Ada and the Menominee. I accompanied tribal representatives to Washington, D.C. We lobbied to reverse the federal policy of termination—a law intended to pilfer tribal resources including timber, oil, and fish by ignoring long-standing treaties with the U.S. government. The Menominee and a handful of other, more wealthy tribes were desperate to save what was left of their land and regain tribal status.

As volunteers, we supported the Menominee by taking care of tasks, everything from logistics and travel arrangements to writing press copy and speeches. As a twenty-something, I found it thrilling to be part of this historic movement. Like many young people without a trust fund or other financial backing, I waitressed at night so I could volunteer during the day.

During that time, Ada introduced me to Nancy Lurie, Head Curator of Anthropology at the Milwaukee Public Museum. Author of books on Native

Americans, notably *Wisconsin Indians,* Nancy put me up in her home and guided me through the process of documenting the Menominee struggle to save their land. The result was a book called *Freedom with Reservation,* published in 1972. As the coordinating editor, I had a range of duties including overseeing the distribution of 10,000 copies to build public awareness and drive momentum for our lobbying efforts.

Our reward was seeing the historic passage of the Menominee Restoration Act, signed into law by President Richard Nixon in 1973. This act officially returned the Menominee Reservation (and those of ten other tribes) to federally recognized status.[14] What was initially considered a hopeless campaign turned into a victory led by the Menominee, supported by the National Congress of American Indians, Native American Rights Fund, and a few of us outsiders.

Being encouraged by Nancy and Ada bolstered my self-confidence and was instrumental in shaping my career path. First as a student and then as a young professional, I was protesting injustices, and that instilled in me the belief that what I had to say mattered. Ada and I remain fast friends. She calls me her sister from another tribe.

These brave women made a difference by speaking out. I didn't know all of them personally, but I saw them testify in Washington, speak on television, or deliver statements to the press. As a young woman, I responded to the power of their words and the raw emotion that revealed a determination and vulnerability much like my own.

Bella Abzug poked fun at herself when she said, "I've been described as a tough and noisy woman, a prize fighter, a man-hater, you name it. They call me Battling Bella, Mother Courage and a Jewish mother with more complaints than Portnoy."[15] Abzug frequently used humor to get her point across. Paraphrasing President Theodore Roosevelt, she said, "Women have been trained to speak softly and carry a lipstick. Those days are over."[16]

Fifty-some years later, I'm not so sure. I've noticed that few women share their unique perspectives. Moreover, women often second-guess themselves and, when challenged, fail to successfully defend their positions or deflect criticism with humor.

Are women who speak out criticized (and discounted) because human nature tends to fear the new and unfamiliar? Or is it because these women challenge our perception of how women are *supposed* to behave? Judging from history and personal experience, I'd say it's both. Women's fear of public speaking involves more than our own inhibitions. We're overcoming centuries of programming about our rightful place in society and what's expected of us.

Thankfully, there have always been courageous women who lead the way and do what's considered unladylike, immoral, and even illegal. The list includes Benazir Bhutto, Indira Gandhi, and Ernestine Rose, an early suffragist who served as the role model for Susan B. Anthony and Elizabeth Cady Stanton.

There have always been courageous women who lead the way and do what's considered unladylike, immoral, and even illegal.

In a time when women were rarely, if ever, engaged in public speaking, Susan B. Anthony traveled the world advocating for women's rights, and gave seventy-five to a hundred speeches a year. I doubt I could have withstood the withering criticism and ridicule she received, including the accusation that she was destroying the institution of marriage. Thankfully, Anthony persevered and was able to see sweeping change during her lifetime—in 1920, women were given the right to vote in the United States.

But it was Elizabeth Cady Stanton who, according to Anthony's biography, "provided the ideas, rhetoric and strategy" while Anthony "delivered the speeches, circulated petitions, and rented the halls. Anthony prodded and Stanton produced."[17] Their partnership activated each other's skills.

One speaker who has inspired me and many others in this century is Malala Yousafzai. When she was only eleven years old, this young Muslim woman stood up for the education of girls in Pakistan when the Taliban forbade it. Even after she was pulled off her school bus, brutally shot in the face, and spent months in a coma, Yousafzai didn't stop.

Less than a year after the attack, this teenager spoke at the United Nations, calling for worldwide access to education. In 2014, she shared the Nobel Peace Prize as the youngest-ever Nobel laureate. It's remarkable to me that someone so young has such maturity and insight. Yousafzai said, "When the whole world is silent, even one voice becomes powerful."[18]

In repressive societies around the world, women such as Yousafzai know they can be killed or ostracized for expressing their views *and yet they do it anyway*.

I don't know how they brave extreme danger to be out front. But because they do, their passion inspires us and their words motivate us. They change the course of history.

Their passion inspires us and their words motivate us. They change the course of history.

Yet today, do women prefer working behind the scenes, believe they can be more effective by speaking less, or fear a backlash? In 2011, Victoria L. Brescoll, associate professor of organizational behavior at Yale School of Management, asked business professionals to evaluate the competence of executives who voiced their opinions more or less frequently.[19]

She found that male executives who spoke more often than their peers received 10 percent higher ratings of competence. But when women executives spoke more, both men and women punished them with 14 percent lower ratings.[20] What the research also reveals is that when it comes to leadership skills, although men are more confident, *women are more competent*.[21]

Other studies demonstrate how silencing women deprives a company or organization of valuable ideas. Anita Woolley, a professor at the Tepper School of Business at Carnegie Mellon, partnered with professors from M.I.T. and Union College to test the value of teamwork and find out whether some teams were smarter than others, as measured by how well they performed a variety of tasks. They found that *smart teams* had three defining characteristics: members who participated more equally in discussions (i.e., no single person dominated), members who scored higher on reading the emotional tenor of their colleagues' faces, and more women than men assigned to the team.[22]

But we're not there yet. Ethan Burris, a University of Texas researcher, found that when women challenged an old system and suggested a new one, team leaders viewed them as less loyal and were less likely to act on their suggestions.[23]

Sheryl Sandberg, author of *Lean In: Women, Work, and the Will to Lead*, put Burris's findings into perspective in an opinion piece co-written with Adam Grant for the *New York Times*. They wrote, "Even when all the team members were informed that one member possessed unique information that would benefit the group, suggestions from women with inside knowledge were discounted."[24] In addition, they wrote that research shows "women who worry that talking too much will cause them to be disliked are *not* paranoid; they are often right."

So while we move past our own insecurities and what holds us back from becoming powerful speakers and communicators, it's important not to place all the blame on ourselves. We *are* making progress—just not quickly enough, in my opinion.

There are hopeful glimmers. In the music industry, 2014 was referred to as the year of confident, unapologetic young women. Singers such as Ariana Grande, Meghan Trainor, Taylor Swift, and Iggy Azalea would never be called shy or passive.

Meanwhile, female comediennes including Amy Poehler and Tina Fey have mega-star careers as writers, performers, and show runners—with three Golden Globe Award hosting gigs under their belts.

In early 2016, Samantha Bee premiered her talk show, *Full Frontal*. After twelve years as the longest-serving regular correspondent on *The Daily Show*, Bee decided to venture off on her own. Her sharp political humor has found a new home and her position as the only female late-night television host has the potential for great influence. Yet it's no accident that in her very first episode, she includes a skit where reporters only ask what it's like being a woman in a world of male talk-show hosts.[25] In a February 14, 2016, interview in the *New York Times Magazine*, Bee was asked: "Which do you think men find more threatening: a funny woman or an angry woman?" Note her response: "I think angry women are so easy to dismiss as crazy or shrill. It's harder to dismiss a funny woman."[26] Amen, sister.

There is a top-ten list of female TED speakers, which means women are well represented when it comes to conveying innovative ideas, insights, and experiences. Two of my favorites are Dr. Jill Bolte Taylor's speech "Stroke of Insight," about surviving a massive stroke,[27] and researcher Brené Brown's presentation, "The Power of Vulnerability." Brown has a genuine, self-effacing quality that makes her easy to listen to and helps her connect with an audience. Her statement "Maybe stories are data with a soul" beautifully combines art and science.[28]

According to a 2012 study conducted by the *Los Angeles Times*, women make up only 18 percent of producers in the Academy of Motion Picture Arts and Sciences.[29] Young women take their cues from movies on career choices, fashion, role models, and what's *cool*. Did you ever wonder why there are so few multidimensional female characters and heroines in movies? The answer lies in the paucity of women producers, directors, and writers. When women's voices are limited, the trickle-down effect can affect generations.

When women's voices are limited, the trickle-down effect can affect generations.

There's still a shortage of women running large corporations. As of December 31, 2015, there were only twenty-two female CEOs leading Fortune 500 companies, including Mary Barra (General Motors), Marillyn Hewson (Lockheed Martin), Indra Nooyi (PepsiCo), and Ginni Rometty (IBM).[30] Looking downstream at those who will follow, Sandberg was optimistic: "As more women enter the upper echelons of organizations, people become more accustomed to women contributing and leading."[31]

One unexpected arena where women are changing the norm is the world of video games. In January 2016, women outnumbered men in the University of Southern California's graduate video-game design program—rated number one in the United States. Tracy Fullerton, a game designer and director of the Joint USC Games Program, who oversees this curriculum, said, "Young women need characters to have as role models . . . It's important. The more that games become a key medium, the more important it becomes for this to happen."[32]

As we continue to claim our rightful place in the world and enlist followers through our impassioned words, I'm hopeful that Sandberg's prediction becomes reality. In my twenties and thirties, I chose a career in film directing because I believed it was the best way to deliver positive stories to as many people as possible. Now my mission is to inspire young women, just as brave women inspired me.

2

EXORCISE THE DEMONS: DISPELLING MYTHS ABOUT PUBLIC SPEAKING

Negative stories we've told ourselves and repeated over time are the primary obstacles to reaching our full potential. When we clear the path, we can express ourselves without barriers.

In my days as a film and television director, I knew the *moment* an actor walked onto the set if she was going to have a bad day—and potentially make everyone else miserable. Her "tells" were a particular look in her eyes, the way she carried herself, and the way she connected with or retreated from others.

After coaching hundreds of executives, I can now predict how female speakers will perform in front of an audience. And it's not what women *say* that gives them away. It's what I observe as they walk from their seats to the front of the room. The strong speakers look determined; they exude purpose. There's energy in their stride. They smile, and appear to have a genuine desire to connect with the audience. The opposite is also true. When a woman lacks confidence, it's as if aliens have taken over her body. There's no fire in her eyes. She walks slowly. Nine times out of ten, she'll grip her notes while speaking as if her life depended on them. When I see a speaker who is prepared and capable, but clearly uncomfortable, it drives me crazy because I know it doesn't have to be that way.

I've been a communication and presentation trainer for more than fifteen years. My clients are executives—from those entering the job market to seasoned professionals breaking into the C-suite (senior managers who have "chief" in the title, including chief executive officer, chief financial officer, or chief operations officer).

Although a handful of women seek coaching to go on the speaker circuit, most want to improve their communication or presentation skills to generate more business, be seen as leaders in their industry, or raise awareness for their favorite organization.

Over the years, I've been fortunate to train and observe women who were wonderful, dynamic presenters. Not all speaker fears and anxieties are evenly distributed. However, there are mannerisms and behaviors that are exhibited by an inordinately large percentage of women speakers. And *anyone* who wants to reach the pinnacle of his or her career needs to identify, examine, and deal with these issues.

When a woman lacks confidence, it's as if aliens have taken over her body.

HOW DOES THE AUDIENCE PERCEIVE YOU?

Although many women are extremely competent and experienced professionals, too often their speaking persona telegraphs exactly the opposite—someone insecure in her knowledge, perspective, or physical presence.

For example, when asked to address a group of strangers or colleagues, do you suit up and become more formal? Does your voice tend to flatten out, displaying less animation and emotion than in normal conversation? Do you bury any indication of your unique personality or expressiveness under what I call the *mantle of authority*? Attempting to become what you think a professional looks and sounds like is the surest way to ramp up anxiety. It can also distance you from the audience, because you'll be perceived as less than genuine.

Attempting to become what you think a professional looks and sounds like is the surest way to ramp up anxiety.

When standing, do you resist moving in a space, preferring to position yourself behind the lectern or perhaps even clutching it? If you do move, do you find yourself rocking back and forth, crossing your arms or legs, and sticking your hands in your pockets? All of these nonverbal messages telegraph your discomfort and reluctance to have the focus on you.

When delivering a presentation, do you overprepare, spending an excessive amount of time and energy on getting the subject matter just right and agonizing over the outcome? Not wanting to make a mistake, do you default to reading or memorizing your content instead of working off an outline? Does getting every word or phrase right have a higher priority than connecting with the audience?

I observed an insurance executive with a death grip on her prepared text as she read every word. When I took the paper out of her hands, she was forced to connect with the audience because she didn't have a script as a crutch.

Now, if you thought this executive was addressing a packed auditorium or conference, you'd be mistaken. She was presenting an overview of her services at a workshop of only eight colleagues—but still thought she needed her *security blanket* to come across as a seasoned professional.

Although young women today can feel more equality and respect than baby boomers, this feeling often changes after they've had a child and are returning to the workforce. Then, like their older counterparts, they feel great pressure to achieve, stay current with their skills, and be the good girl who never makes mistakes. They've accepted that to be successful, they need to work harder and exhibit more professionalism than their male counterparts. The pressure they put on themselves can be paralyzing, but many women don't believe they have options.

Striving to be perfect, women study and earn grades that reflect our hard work. We imitate male colleagues and do our best to blend in. An executive from a major toy company asked me how to succeed with her all-male team. The issue was that these men regularly went out after hours for tequila shots. The female executive didn't like tequila or heavy drinking, but still wanted to be accepted. I suggested that she be self-effacing, mock her white-wine spritzers, and then offer to be the designated driver. Many times, however, the solution isn't that simple.

I've seen hundreds of talented women regularly put in long hours, join professional organizations or committees, and take every opportunity to demonstrate their commitment to career and company. But many of these same women are reluctant to speak out.

When public speaking is unavoidable, these women tend to craft presentations that are polite, generic, and middle of the road. They take a nonconfrontational position to avoid being challenged. In other words, regardless of all their experience, massive preparation and agony over what to say, women practically *guarantee* that their talk will be mediocre and forgettable.

But that isn't the end of their pain. Before delivering their presentation, these women find conflicting thoughts vying for their attention and keeping many of them up at night. Their concerns are: "What made me think I could do this? What if someone asks me a question I can't answer? If I take a contrary position, will I be perceived as too aggressive, too ambitious, or not a team player?"

Although we do our best to deflect negative judgments and assessments from others, the strongest critic often resides within.

If your public speaking isn't as effective as it could be, or you haven't achieved what you believe is possible with your career, you can't always blame someone else. What we tell ourselves can be equally damaging. What we believe becomes the truth. So let's dispel the myths that negatively affect our behavior, so we can move on and resume our path to success.

PUBLIC SPEAKING MYTHS

Myth #1: You're Born a Great Public Speaker

Did you master law, accounting, interior decorating, banking, or fitness training overnight? Of course not. The entry fee in any field requires education, certification, and often a degree. Why do we think that being proficient at public speaking or communication is something we're born with? Or, that the first time we stand up in front of an audience or potential client, we will receive rave reviews? Please!

Becoming a great presenter takes commitment, introspection, inviting critical feedback, making mistakes, and incorporating lessons learned. This is why I won't let a client complete an exercise if she begins with a traditional opening or reports on her topic from a 1,000-foot level—instead of investing herself in the subject and making it her own. As a former director, I know to nip a bad performance in the bud. The last thing you want is for a client to embrace an outdated mode of approaching her material, and have that scored into memory. At the same time, I need to be positive and encouraging, because I am asking the speaker-as-performer to move outside her comfort zone. I'm acutely aware that no matter how difficult and uncomfortable it may seem at first, the outcome is well worth it. And once learned, the new behavior is what characterizes seasoned veterans and successful professionals.

In *Outliers: The Story of Success,* author Malcolm Gladwell quoted neurologist Daniel Levitin as saying that "ten thousand hours of practice is required to achieve the level of mastery associated with being a *world-class* expert—in anything."[33] Fortunately, it doesn't take 10,000 hours to become a great communicator. As a trainer, I've seen vast improvement in only a few sessions or workshops. Because many standard business presentations are truly awful, the bar is set so low that even small differences can make speakers noticeably better than everyone else. Trust me—if you have an important presentation coming up, you'll be motivated to improve quickly.

This process brings back memories of alpine skiing. I had a real attitude about anyone who preferred downhill over cross-country. My arrogance was obnoxious. I'd hold forth that the sport of downhill skiing—if you could call it a sport—was more style than substance. Besides, if you wanted exercise, why ride a chair to the top of a mountain and let gravity escort you downhill?

But whenever I went cross-country skiing, I'd purposely seek out the highest hill, ski straight down, and then herringbone up to the top, just to ski down again. My friends laughed and asked me why I didn't put on real skis and find a real mountain. When I finally took their advice and skied down a run at Purgatory Resort in Durango, Colorado, I couldn't believe how much fun it was. That first morning I made fifteen runs on beginner trails. After lunch, and a couple of glasses of wine, my friends persuaded me to tackle intermediate slopes.

As I took the chairlift up the mountain, I knew I was in trouble. The enormous moguls were terrifying, the slope was incredibly steep, and huge patches were covered in ice. I managed to get off the chair and stand at the top of the run. But without lessons, I had no idea how to navigate the mountain or use the edges of my skis to turn or slow myself down. My heart pounded in my ears, and the fear was palpable. My whole body stiffened, even though I knew that would only increase the possibility of injury.

Fear is a monstrous inhibitor, whether you're facing a steep slope or a critical presentation. It can shut you down or persuade you to avoid a new experience. One of the biggest obstacles holding women back when it comes to public speaking is anxiety. If you avoid speaking because your heart pumps faster, your mouth goes dry, or your brain tells you to *run,* the fear will keep you from reaching your full potential. Consequently, it's all the more satisfying when you face your fears head-on.

If you avoid speaking because your heart pumps faster, your mouth goes dry, or your brain tells you to *run,* the fear will keep you from reaching your full potential.

There's something exhilarating about being on the edge, not totally in control, yet so focused that the problems of the world fade away. That afternoon, on my first intermediate run, I made it to the bottom, a bit bruised and battered but in one piece. And I committed to learning the necessary skills so that I could ski more challenging slopes and enjoy the experience.

Over the next few years, with instruction and lots of practice, I became a capable intermediate skier. Had I stayed on the bunny slope and never pushed myself, I would have missed some of the greatest memories of my life.

To become outstanding presenters, we need to push ourselves to take risks—even if we sometimes fail. That includes giving a talk without Power-Point, speaking extemporaneously (or with only a few minutes to prepare), and moving from behind the lectern to face the audience with nothing between us and them.

Start by making simple changes. Since the audience pays attention to verbs, make a conscious effort to incorporate strong, active verbs when engaging an audience, describing your process, or telling a story. For example, "helped," "worked with," "assisted," and "tried" are weak verbs. We can't picture their function, and we don't associate them with definitive, decisive actions. Stronger verbs include "implemented," "designed," "executed," and "persuaded." Use active verbs to be seen as a powerful professional.

Clients tell me they often use general, imprecise words or phrases to be polite and inclusive, or because they believe the audience understands their meaning. But unless the listener can picture what it is you're saying, I guarantee that you'll lose their attention. Just because *you* think you're clear doesn't mean that anyone else has the same idea or definition of a concept. Define terms that might be unfamiliar to someone in the audience. Use concrete language and visual specifics to describe your concept, product, or services. For example, can you picture "opportunity," "creative problem solving," "brand," or "the vision for your company?" Exactly. So the next time you hear yourself use a generality, follow it up with "like," "such as," or "for example." In the future, replace every generality with a specific example. When we *see* it, we're much more likely to *believe* it.

Once you commit to incorporating new techniques into your speaking, you can take a page from *Blink: The Power of Thinking Without Thinking* by Malcolm Gladwell. He wrote that individuals who are seen as quick thinkers or have rapid cognition employ "training, rules, and rehearsal."[34]

I've yet to meet *anyone* who was born a great speaker. But I've coached and trained hundreds of professionals who approach speaking as a learned skill they can always upgrade and improve.

Use concrete language and visual specifics to describe your concept, product, or services.

Myth #2: Only Experts Deserve to Speak in Public, and I'm Not One

Becoming an expert is a time-consuming, arduous process that only a select few achieve in their respective fields. I applaud experts. But I don't want or need to become one. Although every industry employs experts for research and analysis, we typically don't form strategic alliances with them. And in my experience, few experts rise to the top of organizations.

In addition, I've rarely listened to an expert who succeeded in persuading an audience, especially when the goal was to influence others to take an action or change their behavior. Experts are known for being objective, fact-based, and analytical, so their presentations tend to appeal to the intellect. After all, it's an expert's job to inform, educate, and convey information.

Of course, education and information can comprise a *portion* of any talk, but not its entirety. It's crucial that you carefully select which data to incorporate, choosing only what supports your argument or premise, rather than rattling off figures and statistics that bore or cause the audience to feel overloaded by too much information.

Also, an exclusively objective talk doesn't include the speaker's opinions. As an expert, the presenter carefully builds a case and reports the facts or supporting arguments without featuring her perspective. Interestingly, when a speaker does take on the role of an expert, she's asking the audience to debate, question, and even disagree with the content she presents. In psychology, this is called "priming."[35] Is it any wonder that women who strive to be experts are fearful of how they'll be perceived? It's like encouraging an audience to mentally (and sometimes verbally) tear apart your content. Talk about pressure!

Instead, when a speaker commits to convincing her audience, there are a myriad of tools she can employ. She can be passionate about her topic. She can target her comments to what is relevant to her audience. She can tell stories. And she can add her own perspective based on her experience, observations, or beliefs.

When you choose a role other than expert, it doesn't matter if someone disagrees with you. It's only one person's opinion versus yours. I've enjoyed listening to great speakers who are competitive, goal-oriented, and intentional. They understand how these traits serve them. These same traits have to be subsumed if you take on the role of an expert. And of course, there will *always* be someone smarter or more experienced than you.

The good news is that most of the boring, long, and forgettable presentations I've listened to were delivered by speakers who believed they needed to be an expert before they had the right to address an audience. Don't make that mistake. Take the pressure off yourself. You and your audience will be grateful.

Myth #3: It's Unprofessional to Include My Values, Experience, or Perspective When Presenting a Business Topic

Somewhere along the line, it became pro forma to leave our opinion or perspective out of presentations, essays, and negotiations. I think habit and the fear of being judged drives this condition for women.

Perhaps it was passed down from one generation of business executives to the next. Or we copied speakers who were cautious or boring. Or we didn't want to be challenged. Regardless of where we learned it, we accepted the message that to be taken seriously, we needed to be as objective as possible. This form of communication no longer serves us.

When training women clients, I carefully listen for how they assemble their content. If they go on too long or sound as if they're delivering a clinical report on their topic, I'll interject and ask for an "I" statement. It's valuable for the speaker to include her perspective or tell me why she took a particular course of action. Including your take on a subject is *not* self-aggrandizing. When a speaker shares her unique perspective, the audience understands why it's important to her and will more readily buy in.

When a speaker shares her unique perspective, the audience understands why it's important to her and will more readily buy in.

There was a study conducted in the mid-1990s that's still relevant today. Published as *Self-Presentation Impression Management and Interpersonal Behavior*, the study by Mark R. Leary determined the two most important factors required for a speaker to achieve a high likability quotient.[36] The first is that the speaker needs to reveal something about herself (or her perspective) in her opening remarks. And the second is that her presentation should be tailored or customized to the audience.[37]

What fascinates me about this study is that even when someone disagrees with you, she'll be more receptive if you risked sharing your take on the subject. I've noticed, whether the topic is economics, women's health, or immigration, when a speaker presents a compelling, well-constructed argument and includes her own perspective, she has my attention. I'm impressed (and more easily swayed) because she's courageous enough to take a public stand. In other words, I like her more.

Women have told me that their challenge is to be seen as respected professionals. As a result, they're fearful that revealing something about their experience or perspective will somehow reduce their credibility. It's the opposite. When you open up and give your opinion—as long as it's thoughtful and relevant to the topic—you're more likable, you'll be taken seriously, and you'll be seen as a leader. Here's an example of a client we worked with at Eloqui who wanted to move into upper management.

> **Bobbie*** *was an analyst for one of the world's largest technology firms. She came to us because she hadn't been promoted in years and she felt that her career had stalled.*
>
> *Every month, Bobbie was responsible for delivering the numbers and reporting on the effectiveness of two payment-process systems so her superiors could decide which to roll out to their customers.*
>
> *Over five coaching sessions, we did our best to persuade Bobbie that in addition to delivering the numbers, she should include her professional opinion. Bobbie wouldn't budge. She argued that we "didn't understand her technology firm and advocating for one position over the other just wasn't done."*
>
> *When we finally convinced her that she had nothing to lose, Bobbie gave her supervisors a compelling argument about why, from her perspective, one system was preferred over the other. One month later, Bobbie was promoted to a managerial position.*
>
> *All this time, her superiors had been waiting for Bobbie to express her opinion and take a stand—they wanted to be sure she was capable of leading.*

I understand Bobbie's dilemma. We've worked at companies where the corporate culture doesn't support or encourage innovation—except within extremely narrow parameters. I'm paraphrasing, but the thinking goes something like this: "There is the (company name) way. The company has a template to be followed for career advancement. There is a specific profile of what an executive looks and sounds like at the company." If there's no flexibility in how you communicate your message, it's worth asking yourself whether the company you're at is the best place for you to grow and develop your unique skills.

There's another compelling reason for adding your own perspective or experience, especially at the beginning of a talk. Speaker anxiety typically peaks a couple of minutes before and during the first few minutes of a

---

*   Stories in this book are based on real experiences, but client names and other identifiers have been changed to protect individuals' privacy.

presentation. One of the best ways to mitigate anxiety is to speak about something from your own experience that you know well.

One of the best ways to mitigate anxiety is to speak about something from your own experience.

A few years ago, I was asked to address the Ventura, California, chapter of the National Association of Women Business Owners about finding your authentic voice. The event was held at the Ronald Reagan Presidential Library in Simi Valley, California, and was the first time I'd be delivering a keynote without my partner, David. I was comfortable with our tag-team routine, but going solo was new territory. Even though I was familiar with performance techniques to reduce anxiety, I worried that a quavering voice might plague me.

For my opening, I decided to tell the story of the first time I went skydiving. The rationale was that if my voice shook or my throat went dry, I could easily fold those symptoms into what it felt like before a jump. Every speaker needs a safety net.

While still in my seat, I mentally took myself back to the experience so that I could convey the immediacy of the jump. Even though it was many years ago, I felt the knot in my gut, heard the sound of the howling wind in the open cockpit, and saw the brightly colored parachutes of those who jumped before me. I knew that recalling these sense memories would give my opening story an added richness.

Just as I took the stage, lunch was served.

Without the expected wind-up of "Thank you for having me" or "Let me tell you a story," I started with:

"The noise was deafening. The wind howled. Being the smallest, I was last in line. I scooted on my butt toward the giant gaping plane door . . ."

All the clanging of silverware abruptly stopped. I had the audience's attention. They were surprised at how I started, and curious about what I would say next.

I felt an immediate confidence boost, and the synapses in my brain fired. Rather than getting every word right, I made the audience picture what it was like jumping out of a plane. Once they could imagine it, I made the link with how skydiving is similar to overcoming a fear of public speaking and finding your authentic voice.

This speech was a turning point for me. During the rest of my presentation, I was excited, not anxious. Rather than striving to be perfect, I redirected my attention to the audience to connect and convince them that they, too, could experience what I had. Of all the comments I received after the forty-five-minute talk, the majority were about skydiving and how the women couldn't imagine making the jump—but they *could* imagine public speaking because at least it wouldn't kill them! Even though it was my story, it touched a nerve with the audience.

Myth #4: It's Not Ladylike to Rock the Boat

Don't let fear prevent you from challenging the norm or consensus.

Years ago, a few television series experimented with alternatives to self-contained programs that wrapped up each episode's narrative arc at the end of thirty or sixty minutes. Back in 1981 the series *Hill Street Blues* pioneered the concept of character-driven dramatic television. Over multiple episodes, the show's creators broke the mold by fracturing linear story lines, exploring the flawed characters' lives, and depicting a gritty urban environment. The series won twenty-six Emmy Awards.

The writer David Milch, who also co-created *NYPD Blue*, told the *New York Times*, "There's a saying in all writers' rooms—it's either fear or faith. You're either trying to satisfy your guess about other people's expectations, or you're working through the genuine and authentic possibilities of the material."[38]

By choosing the latter, Milch, his partner Steven Bochco, and others exhibited chutzpah with their willingness to risk millions of dollars and their careers. Standard operating theory in the entertainment industry is to create material with an eye on audience expectations, and typically repeat what has worked in the past. Today, whether it's *Penny Dreadful, Billions,* or my favorite series, *Ray Donovan*, many shows now continue storylines and character arcs over multiple episodes. And they use teaser clips to entice audiences to watch next time.

Unfortunately, in the entertainment industry, there are still few opportunities for women to direct television or films. As of 2015 only 18 percent of first-time episodic television directors were female.[39] Recently, the Directors Guild Association reported that only 6.4 percent of the 347 feature films released in 2013 and 2014 were directed by women, and just 3 percent of the 212 films with U.S. domestic box-office grosses greater than $10 million were helmed by women.[40] There are even fewer examples of women directing *action* films, since that's typically considered a man's territory.

But a handful of female directors have broken the mold. I cheered when Kathryn Bigelow won an Academy Award for Best Director in 2010 for *The Hurt Locker*.[41] Bigelow was the first female director in history to win this award. I applauded the decision to have Kimberly Peirce direct the remake of the cult favorite *Carrie* in 2013 with a $30 million budget.[42] And although the Academy of Motion Pictures didn't nominate Ava DuVernay for her direction of *Selma*, the movie about the Rev. Dr. Martin Luther King Jr., I appreciated the bold move of giving the storytelling responsibility of this film to a relative newcomer.[43]

Most people don't know that DuVernay was rejected seven times by the Sundance Institute before she broke through and won the festival's directing award with *Middle of Nowhere*. I appreciated her frankness when, giving a talk on women in Hollywood, she said, "So often in this industry we wait for permission. We wait for someone to tell us it's OK to do something. Sometimes you have to create your own systems, your own structure."[44] DuVernay did just that when she founded the African-American Film Festival Releasing Movement in 2011 to distribute black independent films. She didn't wait for anyone to hand her anything.

In business, male executives are *expected* to make changes. I've coached many male CEOs and managing partners who are exhilarated when given the chance to put their own stamp on a project. They're competitive and want to be acknowledged for their bold moves. They know that what's risky and trend-setting today may be tame and the new norm in just a few years.

Does the same standard apply to female executives? Ursula Burns, CEO of Xerox and the first African-American woman to run a Fortune 500 company, has an unaffected, no-nonsense presentation style. Her message on telling it like it is can be a beacon for women: "I realized I was more convincing to myself and to the people who were listening when I actually said what I thought, versus what I thought people wanted to hear me say."[45]

Burns also uses wit and self-effacing humor to play down her accomplishments. "One of the things that I was told early on is that you should never let them see you sweat. I remember hearing that and saying: 'Oh my God! I think that they have to see you sweat.'"[46]

Lori Garver, former deputy administrator of the National Aeronautics and Space Administration (NASA), is another woman who has the courage to make tough and often unpopular changes. Garver shared her perspective in *Stop Playing Safe: Rethink Risk. Unlock the Power of Courage. Achieve Outstanding Success,* by Margie Warrell: "People have grown to understand that they know exactly where they stand with me."[47] She didn't say that her colleagues always *liked* where she stood on issues, but at least there was no confusion.

Myth #5: Women Are More Effective Behind the Scenes

When David and I conduct interactive public workshops or trainings within companies, 90 percent of the time the men volunteer first. Women will participate eventually, but only after reading the room. I've even had to "voluntell" some women to be out front. If I had to guess the reason for this reluctance, I'd say it's that women tend to avoid being impetuous. Women don't want to put themselves out there and do it wrong. They've internalized the expectation that if they can't be perfect, then they don't want to be exposed, vulnerable, or subject to criticism.

The only time I see women go first is with an exercise that gives participants seven ways to close a presentation. The instructions are that if someone else has chosen the closing device you wanted, and speaks before you do, that choice is now off the table. Since women prepare as much as possible and typically don't like being put on the spot, they're often the first to volunteer—but only so no one else chooses their closing device.

I can't think of one valid reason why men are better leaders, ambassadors, or public speakers. But each of these jobs requires putting yourself out front and having the courage of your convictions.

One Friday night our synagogue invited an elderly gentleman to give a talk on the Dead Sea Scrolls. The subject held little interest for me and the gentleman was shuffling very slowly to the lectern. I wondered how to leave discreetly before he began to speak.

Had I left, I would have missed one of the most compelling and informative presentations I've ever heard. His passion for the subject made the time fly by. I chided myself for making an assumption that because he was in his eighties and slow on his feet, his speaking ability was diminished. I never made that mistake again.

If every speaker had a similar style, the audience would soon be deathly bored. The solution is to be authentic and invested in your material. It's fine to admire a dynamic speaker. But if your style is more reserved and thoughtful, then that's what an audience will respond to—because it's genuine.

Audiences can tell if you are trying to be something you're not. Personally, I'm turned off by motivational speakers. They seem phony. Their gestures are often exaggerated. I'm not sure what they really believe. Because their delivery sounds canned and rote, it's obvious this talk is a repeat.

To be a persuasive speaker, engage with the audience by allowing moments of insight and inspiration to emerge. Be present. Strive to come across as connected to your topic and the audience, as opposed to reciting, memorizing, or reading your material. Take active steps to break the *fourth wall*, the imagined barrier between the speaker and the audience. You can do this by crossing downstage (moving at an angle toward the audience), asking a question, or interacting with audience members.

Take active steps to break the *fourth wall*, the imagined barrier between the speaker and the audience.

Women often tell me they feel inadequate because motivational speakers sound polished. So I ask them, "Did that speaker move you? Did he tailor his talk to you? Was the speaker genuine?" If the answer to any of these questions is "No," then don't waste your time trying to emulate that individual.

Thank goodness more and more women are taking the stage and being role models for how to be authentic in front of an audience—whether they're politicians, film directors, or authors. Yes, we're still underrepresented in almost every arena, but the times, they are a-changin'.

In the twenty-first century, female comics are succeeding on a par with male comics. Their social observations and multifaceted characters cover the full gamut—from the raunchy humor of Lisa Lampanelli and Sarah Silverman to the triple threat of Tina Fey, Kristen Wiig, and Amy Poehler. More women are viewing comedy as a viable career, despite being vulnerable and exposed when they deliver stand-up routines to live audiences. Note how many successful male comedians, including Chris Rock and Jerry Seinfeld, returned to live stand-up precisely because it requires a direct connection with the audience and fine-tunes their skills. For the same reason, I encourage women to stand up and speak in as many venues as possible.

Two of my favorite comic pioneers are Tig Notaro and Amy Schumer. Notaro turned her cancer diagnosis into one of the funniest stand-up routines in recent years. Schumer is simply unstoppable. She has done HBO comedy specials and reached superstar status—she won a 2015 Emmy Award for her series *Inside Amy Schumer* and starred in the feature film *Trainwreck*.[48] Schumer finds humor in the mundane and speaks to audiences as if we're all having a drink together at a neighborhood bar. Nothing is off-limits for her. As a spokesperson for millennials, she proves that feminists can swear, shock, and make lurid sexual references while still being outrageously funny and somehow *normal*. What I particularly like about Schumer is that she's redirecting her self-deprecating humor onto society. She's my kind of woman.

There are still too many female politicians from the same cookie-cutter mold, but others give me hope. Take Harvard-educated lawyer and politician Wendy Davis, for example. As a state senator, Davis stood in her trademark pink sneakers and used a thirteen-hour filibuster in the Texas legislature to fight for a woman's right to choose.[49]

Regardless of your political views, consider the ups and downs of Hillary Clinton's career. For decades Clinton worked behind the scenes, as well as front and center, constantly under the glare of the public spotlight.

As a young lawyer, she was appointed by President Jimmy Carter in 1977 to serve on the board of the Legal Services Corporation, which she later chaired.[50] She co-founded Arkansas Advocates for Children and Families to support the rights of women and children and was the first female partner at Rose Law Firm.[51] The *National Law Journal* included her in 1988 and again in 1991 on its list of the 100 most influential lawyers in America.[52]

As first lady from 1993 to 2001, Clinton was excoriated for her outspoken opinions, for her health-care agenda, and for standing by her husband, President Clinton, during his extramarital affairs.

After her husband left office, she decided it was her turn. Instead of returning to law practice, she ran for office in New York and won, becoming the first former first lady to be elected to the U.S. Senate. In 2008, she ran for the Democratic presidential nomination. When she lost, she accepted the position of secretary of state—the first former first lady to hold a federal Cabinet-level position—and turned it into a platform to speak out for women's rights around the world.[53] In a 2012 Gallup poll, she was voted the number-one most-respected woman in the world with 21 percent choosing her and only 5 percent choosing first lady Michelle Obama.[54]

Still, Clinton is seen as polarizing and viewed as a lightning rod by many people. The rap on her is that she's not likable. But there's always a price to pay for being visible and out front.

How do you want to be remembered? And what do you want to accomplish during your lifetime? It may require a thick skin and a short memory, but women give birth, for heaven's sake. We can handle it.

Myth #6: I Need to Be Polished and Perfect to Be Taken Seriously

I've seen too many women overprepare and overrehearse their presentations, hoping this will reduce their anxiety and enable them to live up to their expectations—as well as those of others. Sometimes the effort can backfire.

> **Naima** held an executive position at a major medical-device company. She was tasked with delivering a keynote to her entire division. A lot was riding on this presentation, so Naima hired a speechwriter and spent many hours producing a well-crafted and comprehensive speech. She rehearsed and rehearsed, so that she barely had to reference her notes. She felt ready and confident.
>
> After Naima finished, she thought, "I nailed it!" Her boss followed with his remarks. Unlike Naima, he more or less winged it—moving through the audience and speaking off the cuff.
>
> About a week later, Naima was shocked when the evaluations came in. Her marks were in the eighties (out of 100), while her boss received marks in the nineties.
>
> Although she didn't understand, I knew exactly what had happened. The audience didn't feel connected to Naima. One of the comments was, "We didn't know who she was or what she wanted from us."
>
> After this presentation, Naima became my client and never again worked from a script, only a cue sheet and outline so her authentic voice could come through and she could more easily connect with her audience.

When I see a speaker like Naima, who reads or memorizes her material, I know there's work to do. There's an inevitable *disconnect*. The speaker is in her head. Her eye contact suffers and her voice sounds like she's reading, which results in a presentation that sounds stilted and dull. By reciting her text, rather than speaking in a conversational tone, she is perceived as someone who doesn't own her material.

Audiences don't trust presenters who are too polished or perfect. They prefer speakers who are a bit rough around the edges, speak in a genuine voice, and are doing their best to engage an audience.

Audiences don't trust presenters who are too polished or perfect.

There may be another principle at play. Women can be overly concerned about appearances—being judged by, competing against, or wanting to be accepted by other women. Women more than men notice what's in style. Unfortunately, once we sharpen our powers of observation, women can be overly self-conscious about weight, hair, wardrobe, and fitness level.

These assessments are honed during our teenage years and set the stage for a lifetime of concern. No matter how smart we are, we're bombarded by messages from the media, our peers, and even our parents that tell us we also have to *look* feminine, sexy, and youthful.

With so much pressure, women play into the hands of the fashion industry. Men's suits, shirts, and shoes can last a decade, but many styles of women's clothing are obsolete in one season. Skirts can go from just below the knee to mid-calf to mini in the blink of an eye. Celebrities like Beyoncé, Britney Spears, and Jennifer Lopez have their own clothing lines because they know their fans will copy what they see them wear.

Whenever we observe and compare ourselves to others, nine times out of ten we come up short.

By focusing on image over intelligence, style over substance, and being nice instead of effective, women set themselves up for failure. Too many women believe they can never be knowledgeable enough, polished enough, or perfect. It's time to overcome centuries of programming that says our value is diminished if we don't fit some impossible standard.

Myth #7: Public Speaking Is for Public Figures

If we believe the only individuals qualified to speak publicly are those who promote their agenda, sell their goods and services, or are standouts in their field, most of us would never walk onstage or address an audience.

Many women are reluctant to speak if they haven't reached the top of their field or don't have a mission. They also tend to have an aversion to the idea of "selling." But the old-fashioned way of selling doesn't work for *anyone*. The best way to convince someone to do business with you is to build a relationship, express a genuine concern, and put yourself in her shoes. Top salespeople form strategic alliances that benefit both parties. They're authentic, they're great listeners, and they ask probing questions. Even when it's difficult, they do what's best for the client.

The same holds true for public speakers. The outstanding ones are authentic and genuinely seem to care about their subject. Their tone is conversational, rather than professorial or affected. Audiences feel as if the speaker is having a dialogue with them, even though they are separated by a stage, conference table, or PowerPoint presentation. The best speakers share what's true for them and want the audience to take away something valuable.

What are you passionate about, experienced in, or driven to share with the world? After training every personality and communication type, I know anyone can learn the techniques for delivering powerful presentations. But what transforms speakers from ordinary to extraordinary is the desire to reach more than one person at a time. Sometimes a dramatic event can motivate us to change course when we least expect it, as in the case of Ashley:

> ***Ashley*** *was an accomplished fitness trainer, long-distance runner, and athlete. Then the driver of an SUV ran a red light and smashed into her motorcycle. Ashley's leg was almost ripped off and if it wasn't for a Good Samaritan who used his belt to stop the bleeding, she would have died.*
>
> *After thirty-five surgeries and three years of physical therapy, Ashley made a remarkable recovery. Although the doctors said she'd lose her leg, Ashley fought valiantly to keep it. What's left of her leg is deformed, but bears her weight. She still tires easily, limps at times, and has reflex sympathetic dystrophy syndrome—which she describes as searing nerve pain. But Ashley is determined and hardworking. Even though she'd never been on a public stage before the accident, she's now committed to sharing her story on the speaker circuit.*

Ashley's determination to overcome these obstacles motivated her to conquer her stage fright. Over three months of training, she progressed from a passionate but unstructured amateur to someone who can command the stage and adapt her material to the audience. She has become a role model for young people, business professionals, and anyone suffering from physical or psychological trauma. To me, there's no better example of how someone's passion propelled her to achieve what she believed was impossible.

Many women are great connectors, nurturers, and storytellers. Coincidentally, these are also terrific attributes for memorable public speakers. So rather than changing who you are to fit an arbitrary mold, why not redefine what makes a dynamic speaker and apply your strengths to being onstage?

When I directed film and television, I was very comfortable working behind the scenes. I had no trouble directing (some would say bossing) large technical crews, professional actors, or businesspeople. I knew what I wanted and how to ask for it. Being on set was where I belonged; whenever I was away, I couldn't wait to get back.

But if asked to deliver a speech to a business organization, I panicked. To say I was out of my comfort zone was an understatement. However, there was one time I couldn't get out of giving a talk to members of the local Chamber of Commerce on how video could advance their businesses.

For months, I agonized over this fifteen-minute talk. Every morning, I thought, "Why did I agree to do this?" I didn't sleep the night before the speech. That morning, my chin sported a giant zit, and my hair had a life of its own. I looked and sounded like a zombie. I managed to get through the talk, but I have no idea what I said.

Years later, I was networking to grow our then-fledgling communication business. A member of a local Chamber asked me to speak to her group about unique self-introductions or colorful stories that would attract others to their business. My earlier Chamber speech flashed across my mind, but this time it made me smile.

I still had a dilemma. I don't like lecturing or when people lecture me. Yet that was what I'd been asked to do. My instinct was to coach listeners to rethink how they introduced themselves or described their services. I remembered the old axiom from the film business: "Never work with kids, dogs, or amateurs." Still, my gut said I could make it work.

That morning, I gave a brief opening on how to set yourself or your firm apart with a self-introduction and did a quick overview of the concepts from cognitive science on how to be memorable. Then I went around the room and asked various professionals to give their pitch and describe what they do.

My favorite was Charles, an interior designer who dutifully listed his services and sat down. With a bit of probing, I learned that Charles was one of HGTV's designers, chosen to overhaul a family's kitchen. But the family had disintegrated the morning the TV crew arrived to film the completed renovation. The husband, contemplating divorce, went out the night before and didn't come home. The wife was still sleeping when Charles arrived. After he woke her up, she was in no mood to talk about her new kitchen and refused to be on camera. No one in the family was wearing the agreed-upon Hawaiian shirts that matched the kitchen's new decor. Sophisticated Charles didn't get the memo. He conducted the tour for the film crew by himself, feeling ridiculous in the Hawaiian shirt.

The audience was mesmerized. Charles' credibility skyrocketed. By describing the train wreck that was supposed to be his big break, he opened the door for other professionals to share their stories.

That day I realized my gift is to facilitate. Taking on that role quieted the critic in my head and, for the first time, I felt that I was making a real contribution to my audience. Unexpectedly, I also got the group's highest evaluation for a speaker, which made me laugh because *they* did most of the talking. The best advice I can give you is to find what you do best and then translate that talent into how you craft a presentation.

Myth #8: Audiences Will Judge Me Harshly

The only way to be seen as the go-to person in your field is to speak publicly. I can't tell you how many times someone has pulled me aside and bemoaned the fact that *So-and-so* has advanced beyond her, even though that person is much less talented or qualified. Well, *So-and-so* took advantage of every opportunity to speak at conferences, be on panels, and network in the community. That's how she moved up in the company or industry.

But that's not the real issue. Many women won't speak in public because they believe the audience is expecting them to do poorly or even fail. I've learned over the years that you never know what the audience is *really* thinking. If people are on their phones, they could be checking their email—but they might also be taking notes or texting great reviews of your talk to colleagues.

If you see someone with a negative expression on his face, he could be hungry, tired, or processing what you've said. Or maybe he had a fight with his boss before coming to your talk.

> **Deena**, *an authority on software who worked for the industry's largest player, experienced severe stage fright. She was giving a presentation on a large stage when she looked out and thought she saw several people judging her with negative, condescending expressions.*
>
> *Traumatized, she froze and couldn't continue. She left the stage and considered herself a failure. She retired from the industry and went back to school to become a therapist who specialized in career counseling.*

Deena's story is unfortunate because no one should have to be in front of an audience without a safety net. It's the equivalent of the actor's nightmare about going onstage naked. All eyes are on you, and it's humiliating. And when you feel the piercing gaze of hundreds of eyes, it can throw you off your game or, at the very least, make it impossible to think on your feet or deliver your best material.

Try these techniques if you lose your place when speaking publicly.

First, recap your presentation—even if you're only minutes in. The audience will think you're being considerate, and won't know you're allowing your brain to catch up. Just don't reveal what you're doing by saying, "To recap . . ."

You can also do what we call the *meaningful glance*. Whenever you lose your place, pause. Take a few steps in any direction while looking thoughtful and away from the audience. This technique buys you precious time to remember where you were or, when necessary, regain your composure. It can also make you seem brave. After all, how many speakers trust silence in front of an audience for a full three to five seconds?

Another performance technique when you start feeling insecure is to make your presentation critical to *you*. Amateur actors and speakers vainly attempt to make their material more important to the audience, but that's not nearly as effective as *upping the ante* for yourself. My partner, David, once shared a technique he learned during his time as a professional actor. When an actor wants to make the chemistry believable in a love scene onstage, the obvious technique would be to exhibit desire as he pursues his partner. But, if he says to himself, "I'll die if I don't get her love," then the entire dynamic changes.

Like Deena, it can be paralyzing for any speaker to look out at an audience and believe she has lost their attention. If, at the same time, her internal critic is yapping away and wreaking havoc, she'll assuredly crash and burn. There's no way to be in the moment—either in a theatrical scene or with an audience—while entertaining negative thoughts.

But you can reduce or eradicate the judgment you believe is being directed your way. First, find the friendly faces in the audience. (Readers, when you're in the audience, be one of those friendly faces that a speaker sees.) Rather than trying to make direct eye contact, look at someone's forehead. No one can tell the difference, and you'll be less likely to interpret someone's expression as negative.

If you sense a better way to persuade or move your audience, change your content or delivery on the fly. You *can* think on your feet, especially if you've shut off that critical voice questioning your ability.

My favorite technique is to be competitive. Put your full attention on turning around the naysayers by committing to your material. Tune out any negative energy you feel. Show the courage of your convictions. Project confidence and know that you can't please everyone.

Myth #9: Public Speaking Isn't Necessary to Be Successful

Every professional needs strong speaking skills. Executives at almost every level at Mattel, our client for many years, give dozens of presentations annually. They pitch to partners including Disney and DreamWorks, to buyers from stores like Walmart, Target, and Toys"R"Us, and to their own teams and upper-level management.

It's no different in the retirement industry for **Tuyen**. She travels all over the country delivering presentations to her strategic partners, who include investment advisors, retirement specialists, and certified public accountants. Since her company frequently foots the bill for transportation, hotels, and meals, her supervisors need to see a return on their investment. There is no free lunch for this executive.

Even attorneys, who used to sit back and service clients who came to them, now need to pitch for new business. No transaction is a given, and each and every pitch requires a well-crafted presentation. Although every professional needs strong speaking skills, consider the legal industry, where women now constitute 47 percent of law school graduates.[55] That's the good news. Gender equality stops there. As of July 2014, male attorneys make up 66 percent of attorneys nationwide, while only 17 percent of equity partners in law firms are women, and the women who *do* make partner earn substantially less than their male counterparts.[56]

Is it any wonder that female attorneys are leaving the legal profession later on in life?[57] But what if a female attorney is committed to succeeding regardless of external pressures, failing to make partner, or the many other hurdles she has to jump over?

> ***Meredith*** *clerked for a judge during law school and then interned at a prestigious firm, which hired her when she passed the bar. She works an average of sixty to seventy hours a week and forgoes a personal life (including taking vacations and having children) because she's focused on her dream of becoming partner.*
>
> *After eight years at the firm, Meredith believes she's ready. But to attain partner status, Meredith needs to do more than work hard and win cases. She must be a superstar who also sits on charitable boards and networks to form strategic alliances. Most important, she must also be a successful rainmaker who constantly brings in new business.*
>
> *All of these activities require Meredith, who's inherently shy, to develop strong communication skills and give presentations that establish her as a go-to person in her practice area.*

It's not just attorneys who feel the pressure to work 24/7. Everyone is feeling the time crunch. When the recession hit in 2008, companies stopped hiring, leaving the remaining staff overloaded and overworked.[58] Nearly all of our clients—whether they're associates, managers, human resources directors, or vice presidents—express frustration about what they have to do because their company is understaffed and they lack the time to accomplish their duties. Not surprisingly, giving presentations tops the list of stressful job-related tasks.

When any professional tells me she doesn't know how she'll find the time to give presentations, but appreciates that she needs to, I believe her. If you want to differentiate yourself and advance in your field, you must give talks on your area of expertise.

So whether you're a real estate attorney who speaks on what the downtown area will look like after it goes through a building boom, or you're a trial lawyer who wants to become a media resource when celebrities run afoul of the law (I do live in Los Angeles), successful lawyers know how to give compelling presentations.

> **Shelly** attended an Eloqui workshop years ago. From the moment I met her, I could tell she was determined to succeed. A labor and employment attorney, Shelly represented business owners. She counseled them on everything from employee hiring and firing to how to avoid sexual-harassment claims.
>
> Shelly didn't have the high level of speaker anxiety that I typically see with women. She was active in her community—she sat on corporate boards and spoke at fundraisers for the organizations she chaired. She came to us to increase her effectiveness, become more visible, and be promoted within her firm to achieve a commensurate salary.
>
> Five years later, Shelly returned for more training. She brought her law partner, Jim, to sharpen their skills presenting as a team. She also hired a marketing consultant to feature her accomplishments at the annual review. I remember her disappointment when her firm failed to increase her compensation package.
>
> But Shelly didn't let their decision hold her back. Within eight months, she and Jim set up their own firm. To build their business, they gave free seminars and invited existing and potential clients.
>
> Two years after opening their doors, the firm has more than 1,000 clients. Shelly and Jim have added six attorneys and are enlarging their offices for the third time. Their entire business model for attracting new clients comes from speaking in the community.

Myth #10: I Can Play It Safe and Still Achieve My Goals

After fifteen years of running Eloqui, David and I frequently deliver keynotes at conferences and retreats. Our clients come from industries including information technology, insurance, legal, energy, and manufacturing. We certainly aren't authorities in any of these fields.

But that's not why we're brought in. Rather, companies hire us to address employees' communication challenges and provide them with practical and useful tools. Sometimes what we say is controversial, especially when we tell them that the traditional method of communication is boring, no longer effective, and a waste of time.

I'm not a Pollyanna. I understand that I might be criticized for taking a counterintuitive or unpopular position. This is the price I pay for standing up and speaking out. But it's often difficult for women to be seen as leaders *and* liked.

Whenever we take a stand, we need to be prepared to be praised or panned. Granted, few individuals would criticize us if we took a middle-of-the-road stance or if we weren't perceived as a threat. Perhaps the critic feels inferior, which is her problem—not yours. There are always consequences to our actions. We need to decide what's important and whether speaking out is worth the risk. For me, I never want to say, "I wish I had . . ." But I also know my decisions have cost me.

After a successful career producing documentary specials in the health, medical, and educational fields, I was itching to become a dramatic director.

I had two choices. As a woman in my forties, I could move to Los Angeles and try to break into the Directors Guild with no connections in the entertainment industry. Or I could stay in the San Francisco Bay Area, not exactly a hotbed of dramatic film production. I chose to stay.

Since few feature films are produced in the Bay Area, I formed a partnership with Dr. Lonnie Barbach. A licensed clinical psychologist and author of nearly a dozen books on women's sexuality, Lonnie had written books on female erotica that were especially intriguing. I believed together we could pioneer a new genre and fulfill my dream of directing dramatic films.

Our first production was the adaptation of a fictional love story between an older woman and a younger man. We called it *Cabin Fever*. This forty-five-minute film quickly became popular and allowed us to raise funds to produce two more feature-length erotic films: *The Voyeur* and *Hottest Bid*.

The films were hot, but tasteful. We employed established, mainstream actors and filmed simulated sex scenes. But our primary goal was to show the romantic interplay from a woman's perspective. We opened the door for series like Showtime's *Red Shoe Diaries*. Compared to *Fifty Shades of Grey* and the racy programming produced by Showtime and HBO, our films would be considered tame—in the mid-1990s, however, they were scandalous.

At first, I was excited about the response our films generated. We were featured in the *San Francisco Chronicle* and other local newspapers and magazines. We received hundreds of grateful letters. Throughout the Bay Area, I was treated like a celebrity. Then morning talk shows around the country and publications including *People*, *Elle*, and *USA Today* jumped on the bandwagon. Some did a credible job. Others grouped me with the sleaziest players in the porn industry. On one talk show I was accused of being responsible for the downfall of civilization; on another I was a savior for rescuing a couple's tepid sex life.

I was unprepared for the blowback I received from making erotic films for women and couples. My long-term corporate clients refused to hire my production company. Only *Playboy* offered me a gig, and that was a low-budget erotic feature.

Facilities I'd used many times were suddenly "booked solid" when I tried to schedule a sound mix or post-production editing session. And the man I was dating dropped me like a hot potato.

I took away many valuable lessons from that time. The experience left me scarred and bruised, but it also made me stronger. Because I was proud of my accomplishments, especially distinguishing erotica from pornography, I learned to step out from behind the camera and verbally defend my position. Eventually, I met and married David, who was supportive of my films (after checking them out at the local video store—the man does his research!).

Since my reputation as a mainstream filmmaker was tarnished in the Bay Area, we moved to Los Angeles. I had to give up filmmaking, which I loved. But because I had directed more than sixty films and videos, and David was a talented actor and experienced corporate spokesman, we had marketable skills.

Together we embarked on a new career: coaching and training others to effectively communicate their message, be confident in front of a camera or onstage, and set themselves apart as powerful speakers. To accomplish this, we created Eloqui, a communication and presentation company.

As professional women, we always have a choice. No one can guarantee how our decisions will turn out. However, there's tremendous value in moving out front, taking risks, and standing up for what we believe in. Perhaps the reason I'm so passionate about my work with Eloqui is that I made erotica and suffered for it. Now that I have an opportunity to utilize my skills to create a lasting and positive effect on others, I'm more committed than ever.

Take the time to map out a game plan that includes speaking as a way to achieve your goals. Be intentional. I've lived my life believing that "what doesn't kill you makes you stronger." Most people at the end of their lives will tell you their biggest regret is the "What if?" because they passed up an opportunity or didn't conquer what frightened them. Sometimes you just have to take the leap. For me, what looked like professional suicide turned into a career rebirth and joyous next chapter.

3

AFRAID TO MISSPEAK: PERFECTION IS A BITCH

A recurring motif for women is the need to be perfect—in our conduct, speech, and knowledge of subject matter. Striving for perfection stifles creativity and puts enormous pressure on us to succeed.

When asked to speak extemporaneously or without adequate preparation, most women stumble or can't do it at all. Instead, when they have to deliver a pitch, a presentation, or a keynote, most will engage in massive preparation.

I've had female clients reveal that they spent weeks researching, writing, rewriting, rehearsing, and then memorizing or reading their presentations word for word. They insist that this level of preparation is necessary: "What if someone asks me a question I can't answer?" Or they have an unrealistic expectation that the audience is viewing them as an expert, and they don't feel qualified in that role. Additionally, they may believe their job security depends on being the best, or achieving perfection.

> ***Ann*** *is an accomplished financial advisor with a focus on female clients. She signed up for a one-on-one Eloqui program because she wanted to generate more business by speaking to assembled groups and be seen as the go-to person in her field.*

I asked Ann to stand up and in two minutes convince David and me that a solid financial plan was the key to a successful retirement. This exercise would enable her to think quickly on her feet and have audiences see her in a specific way.

Ann took more than five minutes gathering her thoughts before she spoke. During that time, she looked like a deer caught in the headlights. We waited patiently. There was nothing at stake. We weren't her target audience, and she didn't need to be accurate with her information (e.g., the exact portfolio balance of stocks and bonds). Still, Ann had great difficulty speaking without making sure every word and phrase was just right.

Many women are similar to Ann—successful, seasoned professionals who, through experience, know what their clients need. But the fear of making a mistake or not living up to their own standards stifles their ability to communicate. The fear of making a mistake or not living up to our own standards stifles our ability to communicate.

The fear of making a mistake or not living up to our own standards stifles our ability to communicate.

Women often grow up wanting to please the people around them. I was the oldest of three, and my mom was only twenty-one when she had me. Later, my young parents enjoyed showing off their high-achieving daughter. They'd drop into conversation how I was reading Albert Einstein (it was his biography, not his theories) or how I was chosen to take accelerated classes. For as long as I can remember, I wanted to make my parents proud. At the same time, I was terrified that my parents were wrong about my intelligence. And I was equally convinced my teachers had made a mistake in promoting me twice. I was sure that at any moment I would be discovered as a fake. This is typical of many high achievers and is called the Impostor Syndrome.[59]

I took copious notes in class, often rewriting them at night to make sure they were perfect and neatly printed. After school, I'd study until I was able to regurgitate everything I'd read.

Is it any wonder I hated quizzes and exams? I was scared to death there'd be a question requiring an answer I hadn't memorized. I was so anxious that

I could barely sleep the night before a test, and then I'd need to use the bathroom multiple times before and during any exam. I puked my guts out before sitting for the college entrance exams and told my parents I wanted to forget about college and become a secretary rather than go through four more years of agony.

The saddest part was that I ended up equating love with achievement. It wasn't *who* I was that was important, but what I *did*. I still wrestle with that demon and set very high standards for myself, as well as those closest to me. It's still difficult for me to take vacations, because I feel as if I don't deserve them since I won't be doing anything productive during my time off. Some deeply ingrained habits are hard to break, but I'm working on ridding myself of these demons.

At least now I'm in a position to encourage clients to take another path. The pressure we put on ourselves to be perfect and deliver presentations that no one can criticize becomes a metaphorical straitjacket. The nagging voice that resides inside our heads is loud, obnoxious, and demoralizing. Moreover, it kills our creativity. No speaker can simultaneously monitor herself and be in the moment to connect with an audience. It's just like texting and driving. We can't do two things well at the same time. The result is that both suffer.

Listening to this internal critic makes it difficult for anyone to accurately read the audience, think on her feet, or be flexible. When you're stuck in your head, your stage fright ramps up and your stress level increases. The whole experience is blown out of proportion. No wonder women resist or avoid public speaking. No one in her right mind would knowingly enter that arena. It's reminiscent of Christians facing lions in the Coliseum of ancient Rome. Few survived, and those who did bore deep scars. Just think how many would have survived if they had had a suit of armor and a sword? As speakers we also need the armor of confidence, and a sword of words to cut through the noise and vanquish the critic.

FOLLOW THE RULES . . . THEN BREAK 'EM

One of the ways women deal with public speaking—when we must speak to more than one person at a time—is to play it safe. In my previous book, *Own the Room: Business Presentations That Persuade, Engage, and Get Results*, co-written with David Booth and Peter Desberg, we cited the success of Brooks Brothers.

You couldn't make a mistake when you wore a safe Brooks Brothers suit. They weren't flashy or trendy, so you never stood out.

But whether the subject is clothing or public speaking, if you don't stand out, take risks, or differentiate yourself, you will always remain in the middle of the pack and indistinguishable from your competition. More important, if the audience, client, or customer doesn't know who you are and what you believe, it's too easy for them to discount you, ignore you, or decide you are not worth listening to.

If you don't take risks or differentiate yourself, you will remain indistinguishable from your competition.

Anthropologist and behavioral scientist Robert Ardrey wrote in *The Social Contract: A Personal Inquiry into the Evolutionary Sources of Order and Disorder* that most animals have an alarm that alerts them to impending danger.[60] Alarms exist for their mutual defense. Ardrey gave the example of the starling flock. Once an alarm is sounded, the birds close ranks and employ a complex set of defensive actions, doing sudden turns, swoops, and swerves. This behavioral mechanism allows them to survive most enemies, including falcons.

Now, when I see these flocks of birds, I marvel at how they can maintain such exact spacing between one another and fly in perfect harmony. There's no better example of safety in numbers. Unlike birds, who need to fly together in order to survive, humans do not—although watching speakers mimic one another, I'm not so sure. For example, speakers will often open with the same perfunctory statements: "Thank you for having me," "I'm really excited to be here today," "Here is the agenda for today's presentation. The three main take-aways are . . ." Just writing these lines made me slightly nauseated. Old habits are hard to break—which is why so many speakers are reluctant to deliver a colorful opening, move from behind a lectern, or present without using PowerPoint.

I often hear, "That would be so different for me" or "That just isn't how we do it here," which is precisely why I advocate changing the norm. Unlike a bird, you won't be pecked to death. If you take a risk and add your own perspective or go against the prescribed way of doing things, there's a much greater likelihood you'll be seen as a leader and innovative thinker.

This isn't a universal truth, however. There will always be people eager to criticize, put you down, and discount your perspective. But here's where brain function enters the picture. Critical analysis and debate is almost guaranteed when you construct a presentation featuring your left brain—the analytical, sequential, and logical side. That means delivering a series of numbers, charts, or equations. In effect, you're asking the audience to question and even argue with you. It's what humans invariably do when presented with an array of facts.

However, when you utilize your right brain, it's your opinion that you're putting forward, as opposed to a pattern of facts. Right-brain thinking taps into empathy, intuition, and the synthesis of ideas. The listener may disagree, but recognizes that it's your point of view. Audiences will be less inclined to question, and more readily persuaded to agree with you.

Consider how we make decisions. Let's use buying a car as an example. First we check in with our right brain. "I believe it's the best car to buy because I love the way it feels when I drive it or I'm sitting behind the wheel. It feels like my car." Then we back up our emotional decision with the analytical thinking of our left brain. "It was awarded the *Car and Driver* vehicle of the year. It has the highest Blue Book resale value and is within my budget."

Advertising agencies have known for decades that the way to increase sales is to make us desire an item for emotional reasons—whether we need it or not—regardless of practical considerations.

I've had female clients consider all communication through an emotional lens. They tell me they have obsessed for weeks over a comment they made ("Did I hurt her feelings?" or "Do they think less of me because I interrupted my partner?") or a presentation they delivered ("Was I too animated?" or "Should I have been more emphatic?"). This second-guessing doesn't serve us. Women need to develop thicker skins. My favorite comment is from professional dancer Sharna Burgess on *Dancing with the Stars*, who said, "Suck it up, princess," when her male partner whined about how hard dance practice was. Most men see business, as well as public speaking, as a battle. They'll often shrug things off, saying, "It's not personal," while women tend to take everything personally.

What if we accept that we will be criticized sometimes, that there will be people who doubt our success or attribute it to someone else, and that anyone else's opinion is outside our control?

I've noticed that the more successful a woman becomes—whether in sports, business, or politics—the more likely she is to be a target of criticism.

I was inspired by Diana Nyad, an athlete who was sixty-four years old when she swam 110 miles from Cuba to Florida in September 2013. When she came out of the water, her first words were, "Never give up. You're never too old to chase your dreams."[61]

Nyad was in the water for fifty-three hours, battling natural elements including surging waves and jellyfish, as well as physical challenges such as dehydration and constant nausea from swallowing seawater. This was the fifth time in thirty years that she'd attempted this swim.

Yet within hours of completing this feat, the naysayers started in. They challenged her speed (claiming the four-mile-an-hour current pushed her along), accused her of hanging on to the boat to rest, and questioned her stamina and endurance.[62] I doubt any of her critics had ever swum in frigid waters or endured multiple jellyfish stings.

We've become cynical about the accomplishments of athletes, especially after well-known competitors such as runner Marion Jones, cyclist Lance Armstrong, and baseball home-run hitter Barry Bonds denied for years that they used performance-enhancing drugs, only to be proven liars. But anytime someone *actually* achieves the impossible, there's an inclination to discount her accomplishments or discredit her with having a special advantage. Whether this criticism comes from pettiness, insecurity, or an inability to perform, I'll never understand how it makes anyone feel better to put someone else down.

As I recounted in chapter two ("Exorcise the Demons: Dispelling Myths about Public Speaking"), I paid a steep price for producing erotic films for women and couples. Within months I lost directing opportunities, mainstream clients, and friends. I was pigeonholed as a card-carrying member of the porn industry, regardless of the fifty other educational films and videos I had produced and directed.

Pioneers have to be willing to withstand criticism. I went back and forth about whether to include my history of making erotic films in this book. My concern was that more-conservative readers will discount everything else I say because of their uneasiness about the content of the movies I made. But I also realize that younger or more liberal readers will wonder, "What's the big deal?" Times and entertainment choices have radically changed since I produced these films in the mid-1990s.

How you respond to erotica is out of my control. What I *can* control is how I feel about this accomplishment. And I can honestly say I am proud of pioneering a new genre of films and would feel much worse if I'd second-guessed myself and never taken the plunge. I'd just like to say to the creators of shows including *Sex in the City*, *Girls*, and *Californication*: "You're welcome."

The next time you speak, assess what will happen if you stand out, give your opinion, or go against the grain. Should you risk it? What are the potential consequences? How much can it hurt or help you? If you play it safe, you already know the outcome. I want *my* legacy to be a rich tapestry that includes erotica, educational films, Eloqui, and encouraging women to speak out.

Assess what will happen if you stand out, give your opinion, or go against the grain.

DRESS THE PART

I remember when professional women imitated men and first started wearing dark suits with white shirts. Our version of *the suit* had massive shoulder pads, tight skirts, and spiked heels that made it almost impossible to walk. We also sported poufy, curly hairstyles, and blue eye shadow. We looked like NFL half-backs in drag. Thank goodness fashion trends changed.

Unfortunately, putting on a mantle of authority for women speakers has not.

Many women believe that to be taken seriously, they need to copy men, beginning with wardrobe. Let me be clear. I'm not advocating frilly blouses, ornate jewelry, or short skirts to reflect our femininity. And I understand that in some companies, there's a dress code or corporate culture you need to follow.

However, I'd like to see women bring our unique sense of style and individuality into our clothing, as well as our speaking. Sometimes we just need someone to give us permission to be more creative.

> **Denise**, *a buttoned-down certified public accountant and auditor, came to see us because she wanted tips on how to engage an audience. She was responsible for collecting royalties and residuals that were owed her clients. In business, she was technical, matter-of-fact, and thorough.*

Those same qualities were ineffective in marketing her services to prospective clients. Denise has a delightful and quirky sense of humor. Once we gave her permission, we unleashed a creative firebrand.

Now when she describes her services, she'll begin with how she climbed a water tank in the middle of Omaha to retrieve a piece of evidence or lost a ring while mowing the lawn and got down on her hands and knees until she found the needle in the haystack.

Denise relishes making the comparison between these exploits and what she does when poring over profit-and-loss statements of major studios to discover hidden residuals. Her audiences can visualize Denise's exploits, and have a much better idea of what she does for a living. Equally important is the impression of how much Denise enjoys her work.

What made me chuckle was when Denise emailed a photo of herself standing behind a lectern during a presentation she gave in England. She had paired a tailored navy suit with high-heeled red Louboutin shoes. Even though the audience couldn't see them, Denise said the shoes gave her confidence. She'd found a way to bridge the cultural gap and thumb her nose at her own timid sense of fashion.

When you first enter a room or walk onstage, the audience forms an immediate impression of you that is hard to change. However, *you* can engineer whatever impression you choose. Don't let anything draw the eye or distract the audience's attention—no large or gaudy jewelry, experimental hairstyle or color, or bold patterns.

If you don't want men checking you out physically, don't wear seductive clothing—that includes low-cut tops and super-short skirts. Take a cue from an actor or a corporate spokesperson, who wants all the attention to go to her face. This is why individuals in these roles wear simple, classic clothing and monochromatic color combinations. Ideally, nothing in the ensemble should draw the eye.

My recommendation is always to look professional. When presenting onstage, err on the side of being a bit more formal than your audience. When pitching an important client, wear clothing that's consistent with the prospective client's dress code (e.g., don't wear a suit to a manufacturing plant). If you have a light complexion, avoid white blouses—they can give your skin a grey hue. Trade your black suits, which create a harsh look, for suits that are dark grey, brown, navy, or green. Tailored clothing is always in style. Select a wardrobe that makes you look and feel fabulous.

THE NEW DEFINITION OF PROFESSIONALISM

Women often believe they need to assume an overly authoritative and professional demeanor to be taken seriously. The problem is that audiences can interpret this as patronizing or chilly, and perceive you as having a superior attitude. The last thing you want is a negative perception, since that will affect how the audience evaluates your content.

I appreciate how difficult it is for women to give themselves permission to be a bit rough around the edges. However, if you want to engage an audience, you need to give people the impression that you're in the moment and that you're always searching for the right words and phrases to connect with them.

This is a sea change for women. We've always believed the only way to be accepted or taken seriously was to put forth unassailable arguments and deliver masterfully constructed, grammatically correct text. In truth, idiomatic expressions and incomplete sentences or phrases (the way we speak in normal conversation) are more valuable than perfect diction, perfectly crafted sentences, or perfect anything!

I've listened to women over-enunciate their words or alter the pitch of their voice to sound like an upper-class New England matriarch. No one appreciates the condescending voice of authority. The best we can do is to sound as natural in front of a large room as we do one-on-one. Of course we need to project more when presenting on a large stage, especially if microphones are unavailable. However, to draw people in and increase our credibility, we need to keep a conversational tone, regardless of the venue. A conversational tone is a core ingredient of persuasion. You can reduce anxiety when you convey ease—as if the audience is a welcome guest in your living room.

However, what doesn't work is the upward inflection, or *uptalk*, that started with the Valley Girl intonations of the 1990s and has now moved into the mainstream. Whenever you end a phrase or sentence with an upward inflection, it represents a comma and implies that you have more to say or are asking a question. If you want to be perceived as confident, smart, and committed, speak in short sentences that end with downward inflections. Think of it as putting a period or button at the end of each sentence. Doing this will positively alter the way you're perceived by an audience.

Another way women sound unprofessional is when they pepper their speech with discourse particles such as "you know," "like," "right," "just," or "umm." These fillers are used instead of a comma to string phrases together, buy a speaker time to think on her feet, or ask for approval.

Are you inadvertently sabotaging yourself by using these repeaters? Ask a trusted colleague, friend, or family member to listen closely and give you feedback. Using discourse particles is a bad habit that can greatly annoy listeners and distract them from your content, capabilities, and winning personality.

Here's a technique for correcting this habit. In private (and out loud), say where you went to school and what you studied. Put your discourse particle after every other word: "I went, you know, to Bowen High, you know, school and, you know, then went to, you know, Northern Illinois, you know, University, you know, before transferring, you know, to Madison, you know." Doing this exercise may sound silly, but it will alert your brain when you use your repeater word or phrase. Once you begin to recognize your use of this filler, you can consciously choose to stop it. You'll soon hear yourself saying it, catch yourself, and eventually eliminate the annoying extra word or phrase. The true goal is to replace your discourse particle with a pause.

The true goal is to replace your discourse particle with a pause.

There's no question that poor grammar in verbal communication or email hurts you. We cringe when we hear clients say, "Me and Bob went to a meeting" or "I don't have a good antidote," at which point I'm always tempted to ask, "Were you bitten by a snake?" Using the wrong word, mangling grammar, or mispronouncing words damages your professional credibility.

Jargon is yet another land mine. Terms such as *best boy* or *rough cut* are familiar to professionals in the entertainment industry, but not necessarily to someone who works in another field. It's best to avoid using jargon because it distances you from your audience if your listeners don't understand what you're saying. If you happen to use a word or phrase that may be unfamiliar to your audience, follow it up with a brief explanation. For example, with *rough cut,* I could say, "the second phase of editing a film, after the footage has been assembled, but before it's edited to its final length." It's always better to describe the concept with simple and visual language, rather than resort to an insider's shorthand.

There's also nothing like humor to warm up an audience. I don't mean telling a joke. Comedy is best left to professionals. Besides, if you're like me, you can never remember the punch line—it's embarrassing to set up a joke and then screw up the ending. But when you poke fun at yourself, you not only relax, but also put your audience at ease.

When you poke fun at yourself, you not only relax, but also put your audience at ease.

What happens when you make a mistake? Does your face turn red? Do you lose focus and stumble through the rest of your material? Do you apologize and ask for forgiveness—or all of the above? Of course, as empathic human beings, the audience then feels uncomfortable and feels bad for you. Let's be honest. The audience really wants you to stop punishing yourself, so they can relax. And your listeners want you to quickly go back to what concerns them most, which is receiving valuable content.

So what can you do when you trip up? First, don't let your presentation be overshadowed by your blunder. Mistakes happen to everyone. Speak long enough, and they'll happen to you—no matter how prepared you are. Get over it and poke fun at yourself. Say something like, "In English that would be . . ." or "Rewind" or "I absolutely need to switch to decaf . . ." Let your audience laugh *with* you, and they'll quickly warm *to* you.

I remember years ago watching a local performance of *My Fair Lady* at an outdoor theater in Mill Valley, California. The actor was singing "On the Street Where You Live." The set was supposed to rotate from where he was standing in the library to the city street, but the motor failed and the set didn't turn.

I was impressed that the performer had the presence of mind to keep singing. The lyrics became comical, especially when he sang, "I have often walked down this street before, but the pavement always stayed beneath my feet before. All at once am I several stories high, knowing I'm on the street where you live—or in this case, the library."

The song lyrics continued, "People stop and stare. They don't bother me. For there's nowhere else on earth that I would rather be. Let the time go by. I won't care if I can be here, on the street where you live." But of course, the performer was still standing in the library—not on the street, which made the song even funnier. When he finished, we applauded for a full ten minutes. I loved his attitude that "The show must go on." The mix-up was unexpected, yet we saw that the actor was having a blast, basking in the adoration. I wonder if they purposely jammed the set in future performances.

IF YOU MOVE, THEY CAN'T HIT YOU

Movement is another critical element that can affect how a speaker is perceived. I've witnessed female speakers standing behind a lectern and gesturing like politicians running for office. The speaker's hand becomes a fist or partially closed appendage to make an emphatic point. When they aren't gesturing, women will often clutch the lectern with such a tight grip that their knuckles turn white. What does *that* telegraph to an audience?

The most baffling female gesture happens when women step out from behind the lectern with nothing between them and the audience. Far too often, they cross their legs rather than stand on a strong base with their feet about shoulder width apart. I often marvel that women who cross their legs don't topple over, especially when wearing high heels.

Other "tells" that don't serve women: sticking their hands into their pockets, crossing their hands over their private parts, or fiddling with their hair or clothing. These gestures telegraph insecurity, a lack of confidence, or a fear of being exposed. They draw attention to the wrong things. Audiences may not know exactly what's wrong, but they'll intuitively know when something isn't right.

"Tells" that don't serve women: sticking their hands into their pockets, crossing their hands over their private parts, or fiddling with their hair or clothing.

The simple solution is to gesture naturally. Use your hands to describe what you'd like the audience to understand or visualize. My female clients tell me they don't gesture because they don't want to be too animated; they think it's unprofessional or not ladylike. My mother told me riding a bicycle was unladylike. If you're not laughing, you should be.

When actors are onstage, they're aware that physical expression is part of the character they're portraying. They use simple, economical, and distinctive gestures to convey authenticity and engage with the audience. Performers don't gesture without a purpose. Neither should you (see chapter eight, "Move with Purpose," for more on this technique).

I once watched a video of myself presenting. When I got excited or animated, my arms, from elbows to hands, formed circles. It looked like I had "propeller arms" and was ready to take off. I was totally unaware that I was making this distracting gesture. Afterward, I made an adjustment because I don't want audiences paying more attention to my arms than my content.

Take a page from the professionals' playbook. Practice in front of the mirror. Smile and be your own best support system. It may feel unnatural and uncomfortable at first, but you can create the impression you want of how others see you. Until we give ourselves permission to let go of old rules, stereotypes, and what we believe is expected of us, we will never be authentic and let our true personalities show.

AM I DOING IT RIGHT?

Rehearse your presentation in front of a trusted colleague, friend, or family member. Poll them for specific feedback. If you simply ask, "How did I do?" most people will say, "Great!" which tells you nothing. Ask for specifics like the goal of your presentation, what impression you gave, and what they remembered. Make sure you give the person the freedom to comment on anything and everything. As Doc Rivers, head coach of the LA Clippers, said, "Good players want to be coached . . . Great players want to be told the truth."[63] You want to know the impression the audience has of you, which is equal in importance to the content of your presentation. This is an ongoing process, not a race to the finish line.

Embrace and enjoy your success, no matter how small. Implant the memory of how well you did, not the bullet point you didn't remember or what you didn't like and wanted to change. Those minor adjustments can be implemented over time.

Embrace and enjoy your success, no matter how small.

Remind yourself of your past success. Most of us are used to going over our failures—which serves no purpose except to create more fear and anxiety. Reverse the process so the positive memories encourage and motivate you going forward.

4

WHAT SETS US APART: PLAYING TO OUR STRENGTHS

Women need to identify what makes us special, including how we are hard-wired to behave and how we construct and deliver stories. Once we embrace these differences, the next step is to fold them into our presentations and communications. This is how we will be most authentic.

THE BRAIN'S HARDWIRING

Are men from Mars and women from Venus?

Granted, it would be foolish to make broad generalizations when it comes to gender capability or success in public speaking. However, in my fifteen-plus years working with executives in many industries, I've seen female presenters who command the room and male speakers who have severe stage fright and are certain that the audience is judging them harshly.

Research on how our brains work indicates that men and women share more similarities than differences, but there are physiological differences worth noting. According to a study from the University of California, Irvine, and documented in the article "Human Hardware: Men and Women" by Gord Hotchkiss, men's brains have more grey matter, while women's have more white matter.[64] That means men are better at focusing on specific tasks that require raw manipulation of data, while women are better at pulling information from multiple sources and then synthesizing it.

Translation: Women *can* multi-task. But according to Arthur Markman, a psychology professor at the University of Texas at Austin, dividing your attention across several tasks is taxing for the brain and comes at the expense of real productivity.[65] "There's a small number of people who are decent at multi-tasking—this concept of a super-tasker," Markman said, "but at best, it's maybe 10 percent of the population, so chances are, you're not one of them."[66]

However, being good at multi-tasking doesn't serve us when we're speaking publicly or pitching new business. For example, you might be good at researching and pulling information from multiple sources, but you also might have trouble turning off the critical voice in your head when you're attempting to deliver a compelling presentation. This condition is called self-monitoring, but has the same effect as multi-tasking. The result is that you might sound hesitant or unsure of your content, or speak with what sounds like a stutter step as you try to process two incoming signals at once. Someone who lacks a singular focus might also jump from topic to topic, which confuses the audience.

Women are better at engaging both sides of our brains when solving problems. Hotchkiss wrote, "At the risk of oversimplification, it appears that women engage more of their brains when they think. Men tend to restrict thinking to the task at hand. Women take a more holistic approach to mental processing."[67] To me, that's both good and bad news. Because women are more holistic, we're constantly questioning what we think we *should* be saying, whether we left something out, or whether we adequately addressed everyone's concerns. Men are more likely thinking, "This is this and that is that." Oh, how most women would welcome that level of simplicity.

Women are better at engaging both sides of our brains when solving problems.

Since the male brain has testosterone while the female brain doesn't, men have a harder time reading facial expressions. (Women do have small amounts of testosterone—it's produced by the ovaries and released into the bloodstream by adrenal glands.[68]) The influx of testosterone from the male brain also explains why men are better able to visualize objects in three dimensions or read diagrams and maps, even if they won't ask for directions.

There is one particularly challenging aspect of testosterone. Mark Flinn, a professor of anthropology at the University of Missouri, found that men's testosterone levels increase when competing or winning against strangers or rivals.[69] So when a woman competes against a man—whether it's in an argument or a promotion—the man's testosterone increases, and he will fight to win.

Testosterone is also a factor when a man is seeking a woman's attention. Traditionally, men who are successful in winning over women are portrayed as bold and self-assured; that is, with an increase of testosterone.

In either case, use this knowledge to your advantage. Make men your friends, your mentors, and your allies. I'm not advocating an intimate relationship with a colleague, but competing with men head-to-head can be risky. According to an article by Christopher Bergland in *Psychology Today*, "In the presence of competition and a need for dominance, testosterone fuels stingy and antisocial behavior. However, in the absence of threat or competition, testosterone creates a fierce protectiveness, generosity and pro-social behavior. This makes sense in terms of our evolutionary psychology."[70]

Have you ever felt that men don't listen to you? There's a scientific reason for this, according to researchers at the University of Sheffield in England. Their findings surprised me: Men have a more difficult time deciphering what women are saying because the auditory part of their brain processes the female voice first *as music*. Conversely, men have no trouble hearing other men's voices, because their brains recognize the male voice as speech, not music.[71]

Carroll Williams, my instructor in film school, worked as an audio engineer in the film industry. He noted another issue when it comes to how the voice affects audience perception. In his experience, women are more irritated by high-pitched voices than men. I've noted over many years of coaching speakers that warm, mid-ranged voices—male or female—are the easiest to listen to.

In an article about boys' and girls' brains, psychologist David Walsh wrote, "Girls talk earlier than boys, have larger pre-school vocabularies, and use more complex sentence structures."[72] This discrepancy in language skills might stem from different levels of a protein in the brain, according to researchers at University of Maryland School of Medicine.[73] In general, women tend to be better in verbal skills, including those required to learn a foreign language. We also have a better grasp of grammar and spelling. But this advantage often disappears when I've observed adult men and women speaking in public. When you're writing an essay, grammar and spelling are useful. But as stated earlier, when presenting or pitching, it's more important to be conversational than to speak in perfectly constructed sentences.

> When presenting or pitching, it's more important to be conversational than to speak in perfectly constructed sentences.

In summary, a study published in 2005 by researchers at University of California, Irvine, and University of New Mexico, found no significant differences in the *intelligence* of men and women.[74] But we knew that all along. The challenge for women is how to exhibit authentic behavior when we're in front of an audience.

BEING AUTHENTIC

Some performers appear to be the same onstage or in film as they are in real life. That speaks to me. It doesn't matter if it's true or not. It's what they project. Hugh Jackman seems like a genuinely good man, regardless of whether he's the tortured Wolverine, Jean Valjean in *Les Misérables*, or the host of the Tony Awards. He's an extraordinarily talented actor, singer, and dancer. I respect how quick he is to give his wife, Deborra-Lee Furness, credit for making his life better—that gives him bonus points in my book. Jackman exudes easy charm almost effortlessly.

Sandra Bullock is another actor who conveys a similarly positive impression. She can play a Southern matriarch in *The Blind Side*, an uptight FBI agent in *Heat*, or an astronaut in *Gravity*. Without any factual evidence, I believe she is a nice person. She and Jackman come across as unaffected by their fame or fortune—another quality of authenticity. Both have been known to poke fun at themselves, successfully employing self-effacing humor.

At the Palm Springs International Film Festival awards ceremony in 2014, Bullock read aloud negative comments she'd found when she Googled herself:

"There's absolutely nothing special about her acting." "She's not particularly attractive." "I can't stand her, she's mediocre."[75] Bullock is comfortable with her acting and her looks, so the Internet comments were more amusing than hurtful to her. In the same speech, she even turned a media-fueled controversy into a humorous situation by saying, "Julia [Roberts], apparently you and I are in a dispute over George Clooney. We talked about this. It's shared custody, and we both are fine with it, right?"

Feel free to poke fun at yourself, but like Bullock, mock your *strength* and not what makes you feel insecure. For example, in a rush to make a meeting you spilled coffee on your blouse. There was no time to go home and change. Rather than obsess about it during your pitch, you might point to the stain and say, "I recommend the chai latte—delicious."

Speakers who want to endear themselves to an audience convey authenticity. Merriam-Webster defines "authentic" as "worthy of acceptance or belief; made or done the same way as an original, and true to one's own personality, spirit, or character." Authenticity is essential for achieving credibility. But it's easier said than done. External pressures include everything from how well you know your material and how prepared you feel, to what's at stake, who's in the audience, and what you believe is expected of you. While there are many ways to reduce the glare of a public spotlight and be authentic, the most effective technique is to take the focus off you and put it where it belongs—out on the audience.

Take the focus off you and put it where it belongs— out on the audience.

One simple technique is to imagine having a one-on-one conversation with the audience, as if you were sitting across from each other at your kitchen table or conference table. Even the largest audience is composed of individuals. Your job is to put your attention on one person at a time, if only for a few seconds.

Then take the risk of expressing your opinions, perspective, and feelings—even if they run counter to others in the room. Be committed to the material so the audience can sense how important it is to you. But don't let your attachment to the content or your emotions become so overwhelming that you cry in public. This is the quickest way to lose credibility with men *and* women. As Tom Hanks's character said in the movie *A League of Their Own*, "There's no crying in baseball."[76]

If emotions overwhelm you, don't shove them down. Pause. Breathe deeply. Focus on what you want to achieve. Soon you'll be back in control.

If you've delivered the same material multiple times, modify the wording and phrasing to keep it fresh. Convey the essence of your ideas or concepts instead of striving to use perfectly constructed sentences. Include vivid details so listeners can picture your comments and run your ideas through the filter of their own experience.

You can also give credit to your co-workers and acknowledge their efforts with specific comments and heartfelt thanks. This is another way to take the focus off you and enhance your authenticity.

My favorite technique is to put your attention on serving the audience with your comments, whether in a new-hire seminar, safety training, or an exercise class. Here's how one client adopted this approach.

Lilith is a firm believer in daily exercise—it bolstered her after her mother died, and it allowed her to lose weight and combat depression.

She's the co-owner of a fitness studio, but freezes up every time she goes to teach a class. Lilith has high standards for herself, and those unrealistic expectations increase her anxiety. Her discomfort was compounded when another instructor gave her a negative critique and said Lilith was ineffective in motivating her students.

I told Lilith it would be a mistake to imitate the other instructor, whom she described as the poster child for fitness, with zero body fat and the flexibility of a yogini. Lilith is painfully aware that her body type won't ever merit that description, so she spent weeks attempting to master the right terminology, phrasing, and ways to describe each move when instructing students. She believed that becoming an expert would take away her anxiety. Her attention was focused inward, on the critic in her head.

I counseled Lilith to put her attention on the class, rather than on the script she was delivering. Her energy would be better spent observing each student and giving him or her feedback on how to improve postures and poses.

More important, I encouraged her to share her own journey, including how hard it had been for her to take control of her life, lose weight, and develop a more positive attitude. I was impressed by her story and knew others would be as well.

I gave Lilith permission to be her authentic self. Three months later, she bought out the other owner, and now enjoys teaching classes at her thriving business.

There will always be students who prefer one teacher over another. It's not feasible to be loved or appreciated by everyone. When Lilith demonstrated empathy and shared the difficulty of sticking to a fitness regimen, she developed a loyal following. Her students related to her journey.

Having a mental mantra is also useful. Before I go onstage to deliver a keynote, my internal mantra is, "They need what I have to deliver." If there's a lot riding on the outcome, and that's causing me anxiety, this simple phrase calms me down. And it makes me realize, it's not about me. It is amazing how often women compare themselves to one another and come up short. Talk about giving away our power.

Stevie was a makeup artist who worked at the same studio as my hair stylist, Brandon. When she came to one of our workshops, I learned that this beautiful young woman had a severe case of alopecia, which causes baldness. During one exercise, she took off her wig. Clumps of hair covered only about a third of her scalp. A woman at the workshop told Stevie that she shouldn't hide her condition. Stevie wasn't ready to hear this, or to stop wearing her wig in public. She was worried that clients wouldn't trust her as a professional if she revealed this part of herself.

A few months later, Stevie visited me in New Mexico. She'd quit her job as a makeup artist and was returning to Jamaica, where she was born and where many members of her extended family lived. She'd enrolled in an agricultural school and was determined to lead a healthful life, spend more time doing yoga, and "go completely green." She also started a blog with healthful recipes and yoga postures. During our time together, Stevie wore neither makeup nor her wig. By showing me her authentic self, she was more attractive than I'd ever seen her look in Brandon's studio.

Stevie has successfully changed her story. Our journey is to choose what stories we tell ourselves, filter stories from the world around us, and deliver stories that will have the greatest impact on others.

Our journey is to choose what stories we tell ourselves.

WOMEN ARE NATURAL STORYTELLERS

When I was a little girl, my mom used to make up stories about Polly Petunia and Peter Picklehead, two siblings who were always getting into trouble. One time they chased wild animals into the forest just to see what would happen. They knew they weren't supposed to be there, but they were having too much fun to stop. My mom would tell me that even though they were naughty, Polly and Peter told their parents they were sorry and swore they'd never do it again.

Later, I asked my mom about these stories. She laughed and said they all had the same theme: good children listen to their parents. My mom is eighty-seven years old now and can't remember what she ate for breakfast, but she can vividly remember tucking my sister and me into our beds and spinning colorful tales.

Our penchant for enjoying stories, both telling and listening to them, comes from infancy.

From the beginning of our lives, "stories are a central part of a child's learning and development," according to an article in *Beyond the Journal: Young Children on the Web* by Janice Im, Rebecca Parlakian, and Carol A. Osborn.[77] "Through stories, infants and toddlers begin to organize events that occur to or around them," they wrote. "They also learn the essential skills needed to read and write. As early as the first years of life, even with limited communication skills, young children begin to share their stories with people who are willing to listen and observe."[78]

So even before an infant can form intelligible words, she might be silently recounting the events of her day: "Mommy came in and sang me a song and then put me down for a nap. I woke up hungry and cried." The baby is using a story to make sense of her world.

Telling stories is in our DNA.

When parents recognize and respond to their children's stories, it reinforces the child's desire to communicate. Im, Parlakian, and Osborn noted caregivers' crucial role in a child's development of interpersonal skills. "Because stories are powerful tools we use to organize, share and make meaning of our experiences throughout our lives, they become a natural part of the way we teach and care for the very youngest children."[79]

Throughout history, women have been nurturers and gatherers. We count on our social networks for information to make the best decisions, create and maintain family connections, and accurately read our social surroundings—just as my mom correctly sensed and fulfilled my needs.

Research bears this out. As stated earlier in this chapter, men tend to use more of the left side of their brains, while women tend to use both cerebral areas for visual, verbal, and emotional responses. Accessing both the left and right sides of our brains makes women better at reading messages in gestures and facial expressions.

Accessing both the left and right sides of our brains makes women better at reading gestures and facial expressions.

To oversimplify, women are more sensitive than men, which could be why we're reluctant to speak in public with everyone staring at us, and why we judge ourselves so harshly. Historically, we've been more comfortable as highly socialized communicators, engaged in conversations, rather than being the solo act on a public stage.

Stories are recognizable patterns in which we find meaning, according to anthropologist Frank Rose in "The Art of Immersion: Why Do We Tell Stories?" He agreed with psychologists who study child development, writing that "We use stories to make sense of our world and to share that understanding with others. They are the signal in the noise."[80]

Rose also recounted how stories have been transmitted throughout time. Initially we drew pictures on cave walls, ceramic urns, and weapons. With the advent of the printing press and movable type, stories were told through novels and periodicals. Motion-picture cameras enabled us to make movies. Next there was television and the Internet, followed by technological bells and whistles such as PowerPoint software and its offspring. But the consistent factor with each new version of visual storytelling, regardless of the medium, is that our voices make sense of the pictures.

Another insight came from a survey by the Pew Research Center on how we use email. Although the results are from 2005, I think the findings would also apply to the more recent phenomenon of texting. According to the survey, "More women than men send and receive email, and they use it in a richer and more engaging way. Women are more likely than men to use email to write friends and family about a variety of topics—from sharing news and worries, to planning events, and forwarding jokes and funny stories—women are more likely to feel satisfied with the role of email in their lives, especially when it comes to nurturing their relationships."[81]

When I apply these insights to public speaking, I realize why women might have trouble editing their content. Staying on point and being persuasive is difficult when we want to share and include news that's interesting but might not be relevant to our specific topic.

Psychiatrist Carl Jung studied story archetypes or themes that crop up again and again and affect the deepest part of our brain. Jung claimed that all of us have "a collective unconscious containing 'primordial images' from the earliest stages of humanity."[82] He believed that studying archetypes (e.g., overcoming obstacles, struggling against temptation, finding love, or returning home) is a way we understand the human mind. His theory may explain why certain stories and universal themes resonate with both the storyteller and the listener.

As a result, how can we ignore the power of stories that are so deeply ingrained in our history, our religion, and our culture? We shouldn't. As Rose wrote, "We know this much: People want to be immersed. They want to get involved in a story, to carve out a role for themselves, to make it their own."[83]

My favorite poet is Maya Angelou, author of *I Know Why the Caged Bird Sings*. When President Clinton was inaugurated in 1993, Angelou was asked to compose and present a poem for the event. She titled it, "On the Pulse of Morning." Reflecting on a lifetime of racial prejudice, Angelou made a simple comment that imprinted on my memory:

> *History, despite its wrenching pain,*
> *Cannot be unlived, and if faced*
> *With courage, need not be lived again.*[84]

There are consequences if we don't tell our stories, from being marginalized to passing up career opportunities.

Peter Guber, chairman and CEO of Mandalay Entertainment, wrote in *Tell to Win: Connect, Persuade, and Triumph with the Hidden Power of Story* that people aren't inspired by "data dumps, dense PowerPoint slides, or spreadsheets packed with figures." Instead, "people are moved by emotion. The best way to emotionally connect other people to our agenda begins with Once upon a time . . ."[85] Having sat through far too many PowerPoint presentations, I couldn't agree more.

But here's the cool aspect of why people need to tell stories. As Jonathan Gottschall wrote in *The Storytelling Animal: How Stories Make Us Human*, "results repeatedly show that our attitudes, fears, hopes and values are strongly influenced by story. In fact, fiction seems to be more effective at changing beliefs than writing that is specifically designed to persuade through argument and evidence."[86]

It gets better. As Gottschall noted in an article on storytelling for *Fast Company*, findings of psychologists Melanie Green and Tim Brock show that the more absorbed readers are in a story, the more the story changes them. "When we read dry factual arguments, we read with our dukes up," Gottschall wrote.[87] "We are critical and skeptical. But when we are absorbed in a story, we drop our intellectual guard. We are moved emotionally and this seems to leave us defenseless." And, I would argue, more receptive.

His premise is that a story has the same function as the Trojan horse. We use a story to captivate our audience, compelling listeners to put aside their critical acumen, sit back, and enjoy the ride. It's also why stories can change behavior. As we say at Eloqui, "Attention precedes comprehension." Nothing stirs the imagination like a good story.

We use a story to captivate our audience, compelling listeners to put aside their critical acumen, sit back, and enjoy the ride.

Executives in the corporate world are taking note. Companies including FedEx, Kimberly-Clark, and Microsoft are teaching executives to tell stories to improve workplace communication. At Procter & Gamble, a single mother's plight about the economic trade-offs she had to make to support her children persuaded executives to lower the company's price on a container of shortening.[88]

Even litigators will tell you that winning a jury trial is all about dueling narratives or who has the better story. Both sides have the same set of facts, but how each attorney constructs and delivers her argument is everything.

In "The Importance of Storytelling as a Tool in the Practice of Law," Michael J. Newman offered another perspective. "When presented with bare facts and statistics, people only become further entrenched in their own point of view. This is known as the backfire effect. Put another way, stories are far more effective than argument and facts at changing people's minds."[89]

We seem to be spending too much time, effort, and energy on making sure all of our facts are accurate and worrying about the details. When we step back and play to our strengths, such as telling a good story, we'll be more persuasive, influential, and successful. (See chapter six, "The Value of Using Strong Technique," for specific tips on how to construct and deliver compelling stories.)

5

READ YOUR AUDIENCE:
THE ELOQUI
COMMUNICATION INDEX

*There's a shortcut to identifying the communication style of whomever
you're speaking to. Use the Eloqui Communication Index to quickly
identify how your listener processes information and expresses ideas. Adapt
your words to speak their language and achieve greater success at creating
influence and connection.*

O ver the years, I've paid close attention to the language and behavior
of hundreds of clients. These observations provided insights into
their communication styles:

- Was the CEO bored, impatient, and ready to move on when she said, "I know," "Give me the executive summary," or "Get to the point?"

- Did the program director say, "I'll handle it" and volunteer to take over a project (even though her plate was full) because she didn't think anyone else could do it as well?

- Did the head of a nonprofit focus on the contribution that her organization was making to eradicating cancer?

- Did the engineer say, "I think the challenges in this design might affect . . ." when describing a drone, because there might be more research to consider before delivering her final recommendation?

We each have different ways of communicating. While there are numerous personality tests and indices that contain useful insights, David and I developed the Eloqui Communication Index (ECI). We use this index to identify how someone communicates and interacts with others. The ECI is based on demeanor—the *how* of someone's behavior—instead of personality, or the *why* of behavior. Use it to identify your communication style as an **Accelerator**, **Pragmatist**, **Collaborator**, or **Analyzer**. It's difficult to change how we see the world and process information, but we *can* identify, acknowledge, and adapt to someone else's style.

It's difficult to change how we see the world and process information, but we *can* identify, acknowledge, and adapt to someone else's style.

Communication styles aren't gender specific—I've coached women and men who reside in each of the four categories. It's important to give yourself permission to accept your own style, while being strategic about persuading someone with a different style. Consider the ECI an arrow in your quiver.

Accelerators

In our experience, about 12 percent of the population can be categorized as **Accelerators**, although this percentage is much higher for CEOs, business owners, and salespeople. Many of us pitch individuals who are Accelerators for new business, to buy in to our proposal, or support our ideas.

When I see an executive open her pitch book and flip to the last page to check the pricing, I'm fairly certain that she's an Accelerator. When a workshop participant jumps up to deliver an exercise with little preparation and no idea how to conclude her remarks, I'd place money on her being an Accelerator. And when I come up against a potential client who pushes me to defend the benefit of our training and only backs off when I'm more certain than she is, I'm clearly dealing with an Accelerator.

Another indicator of whether or not someone is an Accelerator is how she presents herself to others. For example, her desk will be neat and uncluttered—which reflects her streamlined thought process. When you encounter someone who's highly aware of appearances—whether it's her own unique style of dress or her tendency to critique that of others—she's most likely an Accelerator. People with this communication style aren't afraid to be bold, stand out, or bring attention to themselves.

Persuading this communication style can be difficult because Accelerators see a decision as black or white. Accelerators can be certain—despite little justification or evidence—and tend to have short memories of what they agreed to. Don't let their strong personalities deter you. Accelerators will push to see what you're made of and how committed you are. They're naturally competitive in business, sports, and even games. When speaking to an Accelerator, honor the axiom to "Be brief. Be colorful. Be gone."

A few years ago, David and I were hired by the human-resources director of a valuation firm to provide pitch skills to the company's sales team. The CEO, **Larry**, wanted to speak with us before we came in, so we set up a telephone call to find out his goals for the training and get his take on participants' specific challenges.

I didn't realize at the time that Larry was an Accelerator. He called at the appointed time and said, "You're coming to our offices on September 6, correct?" I agreed.

Then he said, "You're starting the training at 9 A.M. and ending at 5 P.M., right?" As I was saying "Yes," he said, "Fine" and hung up!

During a break at the training, I approached Larry to get answers to the questions I'd prepared for that initial phone call. He looked at me as if I were crazy. "That's what I hired you for," he said. "That's *your* job."

When speaking to an Accelerator, honor the axiom to "Be brief. Be colorful. Be gone."

When it comes to public speaking, Accelerators enjoy being in the spotlight and presenting their ideas—even without extensive preparation. And because

Accelerators tend not to rehearse as much as do other communication styles, they can carry on at length without realizing how long they've been speaking.

When a task or activity isn't in their area of strength or interest, Accelerators are the first to delegate. If they don't have that option, Accelerators will learn the details or dive into the logistics of a project, with the full vigor of their intellect and instinct. After all, they're determined to be the best in any field.

Listen carefully to the language of Accelerators. They'll use short phrases rather than lengthy sentences and pepper their speech with "I know" or "It's like this." Their stories and analogies are colorful. They enjoy being out front, on the cutting edge. As visionary leaders, they are persuasive and motivating. They often have a strong following. However, once they create a project, company, or organization, they're ready to move on and let someone else handle the day-to-day operations or details. In the world of Accelerators, new, shiny objects are irresistibly magnetic.

Pragmatists

Pragmatists focus on the outcome of a project or the end result. They make up about 40 percent of the population. I'm a classic Pragmatist. What kept me motivated to write this book while juggling sales, coaching, training, and a personal life was providing a process for other women to achieve their goals.

Strategy and logistics occupy a huge proportion of a Pragmatist's time. For example, a Pragmatist might ask herself, "Did I call Linda to remind her of the dates I'll be traveling? Since there's no shuttle, how will the workshop participants get to the hotel? Don't forget to leave a check for Vilma, because I'm not home when she comes on Thursday morning to clean."

Pragmatists reference the past to better understand the present. For example, a Pragmatist at a major toy company might say, "Tell me how you operated the toy fair in 2015, and I'll make adjustments to improve this year's event."

Pragmatists are also big on value, but it would be a mistake to label them as cheap. They simply want to know that their purchases or services are justified. Another trait that defines Pragmatists is accountability. If you ask her to meet you at 3 P.M. or say that you'll deliver a project by Thursday of next week, don't be late. Unless you have a compelling explanation, you'll lose credibility with a Pragmatist whenever you don't deliver or fail to complete a project on time.

Every communication style has its strengths and weaknesses, and Pragmatists tend to be control freaks. They want things done a certain way, on time and on budget, and will trust only another Pragmatist to accomplish it the way *they* would. This tendency means Pragmatists can take on too much and juggle too many plates.

This particular weakness is one of the reasons I sometimes hear a Pragmatist client say she can't accept a speaking opportunity. She'll tell me her schedule is full; and most likely, that's accurate. But the problem is that she believes it will take too much time to prepare. I'm here to tell Pragmatists that's not the case.

I've also had a Pragmatist tell me she needs to be an expert before speaking. Of course she'll have difficulty making time to research, prep, rehearse, and deliver a presentation, but that's no excuse to decline a speaking opportunity. Pragmatists are hardest on themselves, and won't take on a project unless they can complete it in accordance with their high standards. That's why so much of this book includes strategies and tips to shorten your prep time (see chapter six, "The Value of Using Strong Technique").

While it's commendable to be so dedicated, a Pragmatist should ask herself whether it's only her high standards that are holding her back, or her fear of failure.

Once you've identified a Pragmatist, the way to convince him or her is to use concrete language and the specifics of your plan of action. Pragmatists don't respond well to projects without definitive schedules and deadlines, or to emotional pitches without backup documentation and verification. Start with the intended outcome and then spell out your plans for achieving it. Pragmatists don't like being micromanaged. If you're assigning a project to a Pragmatist, start with the goals and desired outcome, provide a deadline, and let her design her own process. If you're supervising a Pragmatist, it's fine to ask for weekly reports. Don't ask for updates every single morning.

If you're assigning a project to a Pragmatist, start with the goals and desired outcome, provide a deadline, and let her design her own process.

Because Pragmatists leave little or nothing to chance, an event or activity planned by them has a high likelihood of success. Other communication styles may be frustrated by the amount of details and the Pragmatist's controlling nature, but that's how they are wired. Pragmatists need to be careful that they don't always put work over family, health concerns, and their primary relationships.

When a client comes in for coaching, it's easy to identify the Pragmatists. They're the first to tell me they've decided to improve their public speaking and are willing to invest the necessary time, effort, and money to achieve their objective. They're clear and direct, and they have a list of goals.

For a Pragmatist, having structure provides confidence. If I can get a Pragmatist to experience success utilizing only an outline, she'll be more confident repeating the process the next time she speaks.

Collaborators

Another 40 percent of the population are **Collaborators**. They're motivated by the contributions they're making to their organization, community, and the world. Many Collaborators gravitate toward positions in education or human resources. Nonprofit organizations also tend to attract Collaborators. These individuals often measure their personal success by the esprit de corps they create within an organization. I've coached attorneys, financial advisors, and business consultants who are also Collaborators, so you can't make an assumption about someone's communication style solely based on the person's profession.

If your team isn't getting along, a Collaborator is the best person to mediate a dispute. A Collaborator is a terrific listener who has the patience to hear both sides and bring out the details, rationale, or motivation from everyone involved. The Collaborator will find a solution that works for everyone.

Collaborators shine in brainstorming sessions. They love coming up with creative concepts and building on someone else's ideas. They may have trouble implementing the plan, but that's what Pragmatists are for.

Collaborators excel when the situation calls for flexibility and flow.

Collaborators also excel when the situation calls for flexibility and flow. Planning a vacation highlights the differences among these three communication styles. To make a broad generalization, the Accelerator is interested in the adrenaline rush or excitement of trying something new and different. She'll show up at the airport with a hastily packed carry-on bag—because if she forgot something, she'll just buy it at her destination. As an Accelerator recently told me, "There are stores everywhere."

In contrast, Pragmatists will plan their trip months in advance because the airfare and hotels are a better value. They'll prepare a detailed itinerary with all of the sights they absolutely must see—heaven forbid they might miss something.

The Collaborator, on the other hand, is the one who can most easily change plans. Let's imagine you're a Collaborator and your friend is a Pragmatist and you're on a weeklong trip to Prague. On the day that you'd both agreed to spend the afternoon shopping, your friend changes her mind and says she'd like to attend a concert instead. As a Collaborator, you'll set aside your plans and accompany your friend to the concert. You won't feel resentful about not being able to go shopping because what's most important to you is that everyone has a good time. Collaborators enjoy the experience more than the outcome.

Collaborators have high emotional intelligence. They put their attention on others and are very observant. Money isn't their primary motivation. A Collaborator's contribution or effort to make the world a better place is her primary driver.

These traits can make Collaborators quite effective communicators—if they don't choose to stay behind the scenes. Their stories tend to have rich characters, great connective tissue, and positive outcomes. When addressing an audience, Collaborators exude the sense that they truly care. And in one-on-one interactions, they ask good questions and are thoughtful listeners.

If you want to convince a Collaborator to buy in to your idea, appeal to her heart more than her intellect or financial considerations. Focus on the benefit or value of your product or services. Tell her how much it means for you to work together and explain how the outcome of your partnership will benefit her organization. Just don't be dishonest. Collaborators can read a phony from miles away and know immediately if you're being manipulative. Integrity is of high value to them.

If you want to convince a Collaborator to buy in to your idea, appeal to her heart more than her intellect or financial considerations.

Just like every other communication style, Collaborators have a downside when it comes to public speaking. They tend to have difficulty staying on track—they might deviate by telling too many stories or spend too much time describing the emotional states of those involved. They sometimes have trouble deciding on one clear objective or intention for their talk. Getting places on time is another challenge, particularly if something comes up and a family member, colleague, or even their pet needs them. To generalize, Collaborators don't have the drive of an Accelerator or the discipline of a Pragmatist. However, audiences enjoy listening to Collaborators and feel a connection with them.

Analyzers

This brings us to **Analyzers**, the fourth communication style. Whenever you hear someone describing the detailed inner workings of *anything*, that person is probably an Analyzer. There's no such thing as a superficial or quick answer for an Analyzer—regardless of whether the question is about a profit-and-loss sheet, a manual on putting together a bicycle, or the origin of a word. If you demand a short answer, she may comply. But you'll lose points for not using your critical acumen and for stopping her from showcasing her knowledge of the subject matter.

Analyzers are only 8 percent of the general population, but that percentage is much higher among engineers, accountants, scientists, and financial analysts.

Analyzers are systems thinkers. "Think" is the operative word. They love research and finding the rationale for how things operate. But since humans have only so much mental bandwidth, Analyzers need to carefully pick and choose what they devote their time to. If you're supervising an Analyzer, make sure that she accepts or agrees to the premise of your project or assigned task. Otherwise, expect resistance, delays, or incomplete work.

To determine whether you're an Analyzer, here are some questions to ask yourself. When you plan a vacation, do you start by researching the weather, geography, and/or history of the place you will be visiting? When working on a project, have you found yourself lost in details and unaware of time because the subject fascinated you? As a young person, did you have a nickname like "dreamer," "geek," or "propeller head"? When you decide to buy an appliance or upgrade your computer, do you immediately start researching online and dismiss certain websites as lightweight? If you recognize yourself in any of these questions, you're most likely an Analyzer.

Analyzers are the easiest style to identify. They speak in long, seemingly endless sentences. They say "I think" to indicate the possibility that there's more research they haven't yet considered. Their tone is calm and even. They avoid jargon. Consequently, they respond negatively to speakers who deliver more sizzle than steak. You can count on an Analyzer to give you a high-level, erudite description steeped in detail.

To convince Analyzers, you need to have your facts in order. Take the time to construct a compelling argument and make sure you have supporting data. If you want Analyzers to take on a task and do it well, tell them specifically how their findings fit into the overall system, what you'll do with their data, and why you need it. Although Pragmatists and Collaborators trust the opinions of others, and Accelerators trust their own instincts or judgments first and foremost, Analyzers trust only hard evidence or information that can be proven.

To convince Analyzers, you need to have your facts in order. Take the time to construct a compelling argument and make sure you have supporting data.

As public speakers, Analyzers are comfortable delivering technical information and resist "prettying it up." They can go deep in the weeds and lose an audience if they don't first present the whole idea, followed by specifics, visual details, or examples. A fault of Analyzers is that they tend to build an argument step by step without starting with the big picture or giving the audience a reason to care.

It's difficult for Analyzers to accept that the other 92 percent of the population might not grasp a concept as thoroughly as they do. This means that regardless of whether their field is physics, medicine, or financial services,

Analyzers need to work very hard to translate technical information into visual descriptions using concrete language.

However, the Analyzer who delivered a keynote on the Dead Sea Scrolls did just that. Although his age was just shy of the scrolls themselves, his passion for the subject made the topic one of the most compelling I have ever heard. Astrophysicist Neil deGrasse Tyson garners thousands of followers when he appears as a guest on television talk shows or hosts his own series. Although he's a scientist, Tyson's genuine enthusiasm and ability to make us care about space demonstrates that Analyzers can translate what they know into language that reaches a broad audience.

After reading the description of the four communication styles, are you questioning whether or not you may be two of these types, or morph from one to another, according to the circumstances and environment?

In my many years of teaching the Eloqui Communication Index to numerous professionals, I've found that *one* of the four communication styles always leads. We may need to adapt to be successful in our professional position or personal relationships, but one of the four styles resides at the core of our being.

To determine which one you are, consider the communication styles of your colleagues, friends, and family members because you know them best. We tend to gravitate to others who are similar to us. The two polar-opposite communication styles are Accelerators and Analyzers, who tend to have heated arguments, misunderstandings, or disagreements. For example, in many organizations the chief executive officer is an Accelerator, while the chief financial officer is an Analyzer. Is it any wonder they have difficulties communicating?

Another indicator is what first comes to mind when you approach a project, tough challenge, or activity. Is it research, outcome, feeling, or the big idea? Examining how your mind processes information will give you clues about your dominant style.

When it's appropriate, I'll ask someone how she organizes her clothes closet. Pragmatists will have items organized by season, color, and style. Efficiency is paramount. Accelerators also value organization—for the purpose of speed and moving on to other, more important tasks. This is why they will delegate even this function. Collaborators keep things for sentimental value. Analyzers will have a system only they understand. No test is 100 percent accurate, but this one tends to be quite revealing.

When it comes to determining a client's communication style, particularly at an initial meeting, listen to how the person speaks and operates.

Accelerators will quickly jump to the bottom line. They use colorful, descriptive language, tell great stories, challenge your thinking, and have the unassailable courage of their convictions.

Pragmatists start with the end in sight and then fill in the steps to achieving their goal. They might ask what steps *you* plan on taking to achieve an objective. They speak about the value (investment vs. expense) of a service and they're curious about how a project was done previously. Pragmatists are implementers, so whenever you see what my friend Ada calls the worker bees, you're probably looking at a hive of Pragmatists.

Time is in short supply for Pragmatists, so don't waste it with too much background, context, or explanation. The same is true for telling them how you *feel* about a business task. They're not that interested in drama, complaining, or excuses.

Collaborators come from a more emotional place with their language and behavior. They're most satisfied when everyone gets along. Listen for language that supports a Collaborator's team, individuals, or colleagues.

Inquire about what she does in her downtime—a Collaborator will typically say that she volunteers to raise money when a disaster strikes, collects toys or clothing for children in need, or rescues animals. Collaborators can be fierce advocates for the underdog.

Collaborators are creative thinkers who are good at reading people. Mood, ambience, and experience are more important to Collaborators than a specific outcome.

Analyzers will almost always give you context. If you ask about her favorite restaurant, she'll tell you which neighborhood it's in—complete with the street quadrants. If you ask which remote is used to control the television volume, she'll explain how to use each of the five remotes in the room. If you want the sales figures in the Northwest region for the last quarter, she'll first ask what the numbers will be used for. It's critical for people with this communication style to know how the data they research and deliver fits into the overall system.

Obviously, no *one* communication style is better or worse than any other. The difficulty for many of us is accepting that someone isn't wrong just because she thinks, speaks, and operates differently than we do. (Some women even blame themselves when things go awry: "I'm wrong and they're right.") I frequently hear versions of "If only they would do it this way" as an explanation of why an approach didn't work. In essence, the individual is saying, "If the other person had done it *my* way, it would have been successful." What's clear to us isn't always obvious, comfortable, or acceptable to someone else.

We can't change who we are, but we can definitely learn to appreciate and speak someone else's language. (OMG, I sound like a Collaborator!) From my practical, Pragmatic point of view, every well-functioning team includes all four communication styles.

Armed with this knowledge, go back to the beginning of this chapter and see if you can identify the communication style exhibited in each example.

A logical question, after you've mastered the ECI, is, "How can I appeal to all four communication styles when I'm speaking to a large audience?" The answer is to tell a story, which is right in our sweet spot.

6

THE VALUE OF USING STRONG TECHNIQUE

No one has enough time. Add to that, life is fluid and changeable.
Everyone needs structure to tell a great story, build a presentation quickly,
and deliver with style.

STORYTELLING: YOU'RE THE HERO!

An interviewer once asked Don Hewitt, the creator and producer of CBS's *60 Minutes*—the longest-running prime-time broadcast on American television—what the secret is of his show's staying power. Hewitt summed it up in four words: "Tell me a story."[90] He was right about not only what makes a successful television program, but also what makes a successful business presentation.

As a culture, we are raised on stories—from the Bible and creation myths, to fairy tales, novels, and songs. The stories we tell in a professional setting can have an equally strong influence, if they are told well and targeted to the specific interests and needs of the audience.

Whether you're a manager, C-suite executive, or thought leader, there are guiding principles to constructing and delivering effective anecdotes. And the beauty of stories is that they can be placed at the beginning, middle, or end of your presentation.

First, identify one strong message that is embedded in your story. Why are you telling us this tale? What do you hope to accomplish? For example, if you want clients to call on you when another service professional has dropped the ball, you will emphasize great customer service. Or, if you want to be known as the creative problem solver who can handle the most complex negotiations, your story will reflect just that.

Even though you and your firm provide a number of services, identify one clear, actionable message per story. A story with a strong message is the difference between rambling and being razor sharp in your content and delivery.

A story with a strong message is the difference between rambling and being razor sharp in your content and delivery.

THREE ACTS OF A GREAT STORY

Eloqui devised a template for telling anecdotes called the OSB: Obstacle, Solution, Benefit. Using this formula will keep you on track and give you the greatest likelihood of success. And with only three acts, or sections, it's not difficult to remember your structure, and the audience can retain the important ideas. Plus, by following this structure, a story can be told in about two to three minutes.

Obstacle

First, let's examine the **Obstacle**. This is where you hook the audience and succinctly describe the client's challenge.

Following is an example, constructed to showcase each act:

Obstacle: *A custom publishing house in Nashville called Eloqui in a panic. Their largest client had decided to put their contract out to bid. This business was worth $5 million a year. The pitch was in ten days, and they were up against two larger and better-known firms. If they lost, the publishing house would likely go under.*

Notice that I didn't add much context or background before beginning the story. I didn't give a detailed history of the firm or our experience with them. Better to start with a strong obstacle to draw the audience in and make them care. To make the obstacle more compelling, always include what is at stake and the time sensitivity. The goal is to have listeners say to themselves, "What happened next?" as opposed to, "Oh, no, not another one of Jennifer's war stories!"

Solution

The second act is the **Solution**. Here is where you describe your specific process and demonstrate what sets you apart. The Solution exhibits how you operate, rather than providing a menu of your products and services, which is dull and forgettable.

As mentioned in chapter two, use active verbs like *investigate, determine*, or *analyze* when describing what you did to solve the problem. Eliminate *help* from your vocabulary. And whenever possible, include what you or the client discovered during the process. I've underlined the active verbs in the following example:

> **Solution:** *We immediately flew to Nashville and met with their pitch team. We established a common Intention so that everyone was on the same page. Then we divided the material to be delivered according to everyone's skill set: some of the presenters were big picture and others were detail.*
>
> *After interviewing the team members, we recommended that the president become the facilitator while the founder assume the role of Visionary.*
>
> *Then we rehearsed how the material was handed off until the flow was seamless. And once we discovered why the client was putting the contract out to bid, we encouraged the president to explain what the company would do differently should they be awarded the contract.*

If you're part of a team, feel free to use "we" for at least two of the active verbs in your Solution section, but whenever possible, include at least one "I" for the audience to know your personal investment or skin in the game.

Benefit

The third act in this mini three-act play is the **Benefit** or the outcome. This is what everyone in business wants to know. Put another way, "How will your services, plan, or proposal serve me?" For a twist at the end, include the ***Unexpected Benefit***. This is the transformational element—the "aha" moment, or what the client can do differently going forward simply by working with you.

The Unexpected Benefit is the transformational element—the "aha" moment, or what the client can do differently going forward simply by working with you.

Benefit: *The custom publishing company won the contract.*

Unexpected Benefit: *The company's executive team realized they now had a well-oiled pitch machine. In the future, rather than depending on a single client for their survival, they could diversify and go after other, larger contracts.*

Another advantage of a well-told story is that it appeals to all communication styles:

For **Accelerators**, this template is designed to be brief and keep the speaker on track. Starting with a challenge or Obstacle hooks the Accelerator and keeps him or her paying attention into the second act.

Pragmatists appreciate structure. They pay close attention to the process or Solution section, which clearly delineates the steps leading to a successful outcome.

Collaborators relate to the characters and their well-being. The Unexpected Benefit highlighting the value is especially appealing to them.

Analyzers appreciate the logical flow of a well-told story. Analyzers relate to context, details, and how the three acts fit together in a logical system.

Telling a compelling story takes introspection, deliberation, and practice—regardless of the form you use. Think back to when the event happened. This will bring your example to life, make it sound fresh, and allow you to remember more of the salient, colorful details. And your delivery will be more vibrant, even though the event occurred years ago.

Effective stories borrow from the world of cognitive science, meaning that as you construct your narrative, use specific details as opposed to generalities. Paint visual snapshots with vivid descriptors so the listener pictures your scenes as you relate them. Employ metaphors, analogies, or similes, especially when describing a complex or technical concept. Was the impact of your services like a stone creating ripples in a pond? Or did you charge in like a bull fighting a matador? The more we can see it, the more you will persuade us to take an action.

When constructing your anecdote, be considerate of your audience. If you want to persuade your partners, clients, or superiors to adopt a program, tailor the elements of your story to what affects them most.

If you want to persuade your partners, clients, or superiors to adopt a program, tailor the elements of your story to what affects them most.

The following anecdote was told by **Marc**, a labor attorney, during one of his corporate trainings on wage-and-hour regulations:

My seventeen-year-old daughter, Penelope, worked at my law firm over her summer break. She was assigned administrative tasks in what we call the dungeon. It's the basement where client folders are organized, indexed, and filed.

After she'd been working a couple of days, I asked Penelope how it was going. She said, "Dad, it's brutal. I've got paper cuts. I'm balancing on chairs. I've had to change my clothes because it's so dirty. And by the way, when do I take lunch? And can I leave early if I take a shorter lunch?"

While Penelope was talking, I was thinking to myself, "Oh, no. Workers' comp, OSHA, overtime penalties, meals, and rest breaks." My own firm had failed to advise a part-time worker of her schedule and rights. We were guilty of the same oversight as our clients. It made me realize how easy it is to overlook what we are required by law to cover with our workers.

Stories are malleable. You can repurpose the message in each story according to what you want to achieve or whom you want to convince. Call it artistic license.

As women, we need to realize the value of our stories and gain the courage to tell them. Your whole life is material. Start assembling stories that showcase your strengths, target what kind of work you want more of, or demonstrate what sets you or your business apart. Remember, these are *your* stories. No one can debate their veracity, your feelings about them, or what the outcome means to you.

But stories are only one tool in your kit. Whether you're pitching a potential client, delivering a presentation on your area of expertise, relating what you do at a networking meeting, or giving the media a quotable sound bite, each presentation requires its own unique combination of ingredients.

SIX ELEMENTS THAT GIVE YOUR TALK A SOLID STRUCTURE

First, consider why you want (or have been asked) to give a presentation. Do you have something valuable to share? Does your experience set you apart? Are you passionate about your topic? Remind yourself of these reasons when your internal critic starts dissuading you from speaking. There will be times when things don't go well. For example, you may be asked to deliver material you're not totally familiar with, the entire audience may not respond positively, or you may experience technical difficulties beyond your control. When these problems occur, professionals always fall back on structure and technique.

When you sit down to work on your presentation, begin by creating an overview—organizing your content on one sheet of paper or a blank word-processing file. Jot down key words and phrases instead of complete sentences. Be sure to include lots of white space on the page. Then, start filling in each of the following sections.

Intention

Before constructing your presentation, determine what you want to achieve more than anything else. Make this Intention a short, actionable statement that you can refer back to while presenting.

Before constructing your presentation, determine what you want to achieve more than anything else.

Role

What Role would best deliver your Intention? Consider how you want to be perceived. Possible choices include Motivator, Coach, Seasoned Veteran, Facilitator, or Visionary.
Note: Select your Intention and Role based on the audience.

Opening

Dive off a cliff without windups or obligatory phrases. Grab the attention of your audience with an arresting open. The purpose of an opening is to set the tone and the frame. Then link this opening to your topic with specific, visual details.

Theme

The theme is the central idea of your talk. Good openings often suggest a theme, which is a short, easily repeatable phrase. Examples from the corporate world include "Just do it" (Nike), "The ultimate driving machine" (BMW), "Just the right amount of wrong" (the Cosmopolitan Hotel), and "Creating the future of play" (Mattel). Revisit your theme every so often during your presentation, the same way or with slight variation.

Talking Points

When you're coming up with your main ideas, remember the power of three: three is the preferred number of items to include in a list if you're trying to maximize the likelihood that someone will be able to recall them later on. So divide your presentation into three talking points, headings, or buckets.

Divide your presentation into three talking points, headings, or buckets.

Then come up with examples, analogies, or interactive exercises that you can use to highlight each bucket. After you've finalized your talking points, you're ready to construct, design, and include your PowerPoint in the presentation. Whenever possible, don't open or close with PowerPoint, unless it's to show your company logo. You want all the attention on you to frame and wrap up your presentation.

If you're afraid you'll forget your buckets, you can use a mnemonic to jog your memory. For example, let's say the three buckets of my presentation are:

- the basics of effective communication

- errors commonly made by speakers

- ways you can transform your future presentations

I would jot down the trigger word for each bucket (basics, errors, transform) or form the acronym BET to stand for each idea.

It may also be useful to determine how you want to transition between talking points or buckets. You can always include these transitions in your outline.

Closing

Select a conclusion that suits your Intention. Although there are seven options that I describe later, three reliable choices include a Call to Action, with three active verbs; a Bookend, where you revisit your opening with one new insight; or a Recap, which summarizes your key points.

THE CUE SHEET

This may surprise you: For a longer presentation (anything from five minutes to a couple of hours), you can outline your talk in just thirty minutes.

Consider the outline your GPS or cue sheet. It will guide you to your destination, identifying the key *locations* along the way. It will provide clarity if you feel stressed. And it will direct you back on course if you've gone astray. Best of all, the GPS navigational system's voice is nonjudgmental.

Create an outline using only key words, cues, or trigger phrases. We don't speak the way we write, so it's impossible to sound natural, conversational, or invested in your material when you're reading your content, looking down, or using a teleprompter. Speakers tend to sound robotic when they deliver from a prepared text—even if they wrote the material themselves. If your presentation has many moving parts, if there are high expectations that it will be successful, or if it's the first time you've spoken on this topic, feel free to write out your content as if you're composing a report or an essay. Then take another pass and come up with an outline.

The best way to use an outline when you're speaking is to glance down and pick up an idea, key word, or phrase. Speak for a few minutes. Then pause, look down, and grab the next key word. Look up and regain eye contact with the audience before continuing.

When constructing a talk, most people start by assembling all their content, trying to become an expert, or building a PowerPoint deck. Now you have a more effective way. Once you know how to structure a great presentation, your prep time will be reduced. And you can't help but gain confidence, because you have the underpinnings of structure to fall back on.

Once you know how to structure a great presentation, your prep time will be reduced.

ABOVE ALL, KNOW YOUR INTENTION

Intention is a powerful device that forces us to focus, make difficult decisions, and edit our content. I've found Intention to be one of the most difficult concepts for our clients to grasp initially. However, when implemented, Intention can have an incredible impact on your presentation, your career, and your life.

Identify your Intention *before* assembling your content or putting together your PowerPoint deck. Be strategic. Think about what you want to achieve before every meeting, pitch session, phone conversation, or speech.

However, don't choose an Intention to have the audience or client like you, recognize how talented or smart you are, or realize how much you know about your topic. These objectives are self-focused and inner-directed.

When I speak to clients regarding Intention, one response I hear is, "I want to educate, inform, or make sure my audience understands (fill in the blank)." Instead, make your focus be to motivate, persuade, or influence your audience to take an action or change their point of view. Put your attention on the listener or audience and you'll silence your internal critic while tapping into your creativity and intellect.

I learned the concept of Intention when I worked as a director in the entertainment industry. Actors will frequently ask a director, "What does my character want?" No director worth her salt would give actors direction, approach a storyline, or block the action in a scene without first knowing the Intention of each character and each scene.

To avoid confusion or dilution of your message, pick only *one* Intention as your primary objective. For example, when we go into a firm to pitch our services, our Intention is, "We'll prove that Eloqui's services are critical to their success."

With this Intention, we don't list clients, recite our company's history, or try to sell someone on why we're the premier communications firm. Instead, we highlight how we can meet the prospective client's needs. For example, "If you're like our other clients in the insurance space, your producers need to frame the rise in premiums, so that your customers don't shop for a new broker."

We've also done research on the firm, so that we can make assumptions and ask questions during the pitch. We'll only suggest training or specific programs that we believe will contribute to the company's success. Rather than proving our capabilities, we focus on what we can do for them.

When we've achieved our initial Intention and a company or individual has engaged us, we advance to another Intention. Now it might be, "As your Trusted Advisors, we can make recommendations about other service providers who can benefit your firm." (See the appendix for Eloqui's Trusted Advisor Template©.) As your meeting or project continues, shift to an Intention that suits the next challenge. In my years of observing leaders and C-suite executives, I've noticed that they share one consistent quality: they conduct their business intentionally.

When I ask a client to describe what she wants to achieve in an upcoming presentation, I often hear the following: "I want to congratulate the sales force for making their numbers, describe the challenges facing us in the market-place, and have the team commit to increasing sales going forward." That's a tall order. Consider the *one* thing you would like to accomplish more than anything else. This is your Intention. You'll probably discover the other objectives or goals are means to that end. Have only one Intention per presentation.

When a presenter has multiple Intentions, she'll tend to ramble, go off track, and sound fragmented. She'll be frustrated and the audience will be confused. When a speaker lacks a primary Intention, all of her content is given equal weight or value. As result, nothing she says will stand out or be memorable.

Simplify your life. Determine *one* Intention per interaction, presentation, or pitch. Then choose only the content that supports this Intention. Most speakers have more information than they can possibly deliver. Be considerate of your audience. We know from cognitive science that our brains can absorb only a limited amount of material at a time. One clear Intention serves as an effective editing device. Go deep, not wide. Make it easy on yourself *and* the audience.

Determine *one* Intention per interaction, presentation, or pitch. Then choose only the content that supports this Intention.

Think of your Intention as the engine driving every presentation or communication. An active Intention (e.g., to persuade, convince, or influence) is powerful and gives your presentation laser-beam focus. Establish this and you'll increase your odds of success. Imagine how "I Have a Dream," the iconic speech by the Rev. Dr. Martin Luther King Jr., would have sounded had King chosen to educate his listeners on the history of segregation in America rather than persuade them to live together in peace.

Moreover, when you don't frame your information in a persuasive package, you risk overwhelming or losing your audience. If you aren't sharing your recommendation or perspective, then why do you need to speak? You could simply distribute your PowerPoint deck and call it a day.

Here's how to hone your thoughts and shape them into an active Intention. Review your material. If your first thought (or instruction from a superior) is to inform your audience or make them more knowledgeable about your topic, ask yourself, "If I inform them, what will happen?" Keep asking and answering this question until you reach your true Intention. This doesn't mean you'll discard all the compelling data, statistics, or findings at your disposal. It does mean that you'll include only the information that propels your active Intention forward.

Be selfish about what you most want to achieve, but don't say your Intention out loud to your audience. Announcing the purpose of your presentation is ineffective and can make you seem patronizing. It's also old-fashioned (think of an agenda slide) and creates resistance or a prove-it-to-me response from the audience.

When you don't announce your Intention, you'll be forced to employ other means to achieve it. For example, you might ask questions, make your presentation interactive, use a whiteboard in addition to or in lieu of Power-Point, or change up your delivery. You might also tell stories that bring your content to life, which is my favorite technique. Another benefit of having an Intention is that it will reduce anxiety. What goes through your mind right before you speak? Perhaps you'll mentally review your material and inevitably reach a point where you forget what comes next. You'll then panic and say to yourself, "Oh, no! What if the same thing happens when I'm presenting?" Or you think, "This proves it. I don't know my content well enough. I should never have agreed to give this talk!"

Since most stage fright peaks minutes before a person goes onstage or into an important meeting, I don't recommend reviewing your content at this point. To me, it's a recipe for disaster because your stress level will zoom off the charts. Instead, remind yourself of your Intention. This will calm your nerves and allow you to realize that it doesn't matter specifically *what* you say. What's important is that you're committed to being authentic and achieving your Intention.

Audiences can quickly tell if a speaker is freaking out or if she's centered and ready to engage. A speaker with a clear Intention has a huge advantage. As women, we also need to make sure our Intention is achievable. If you're presenting to a room of potential clients, it's unrealistic to think that every one of them will approach you afterward to set up a meeting or will agree with your point of view.

Let's say you're a set designer and a friend has introduced you to a producer at HBO. It may not be realistic to expect that this producer will hire you. But an achievable Intention would be to have the producer refer you to someone in her circle of friends who *could* contract with you or refer you to another potential client.

Finally, having an Intention gives you a barometer for measuring your success. With a specific, clear Intention, you know whether you've achieved your goal. If you didn't, you can adjust your strategy, choose other material, or modify your Intention next time. Women, particularly those who are over-achievers, frequently try to accomplish too much and then reprimand themselves for not doing more.

When a client reports back on how a presentation went, I want to know whether she achieved her Intention. Too often, she'll tell me about her mistakes—that she left out a concept she wanted to include, mispronounced a word, or sped up and lost energy for her close. Odds are you'll forget *something* when you speak. In the end, achieving your Intention is all that matters.

Focus on the big picture. Did you accomplish what you set out to do? If you did, then you won! Applaud your success and then figure out what you want to achieve next time. Let Intention be your guide.

SUIT UP AND TAKE ON A ROLE

After you've determined your Intention, select your Role. Think of your Role as a filter through which to deliver your content. Consider who will be in the audience. Which Role will enable you to be most successful in achieving your Intention? Having a solid, clear Intention and an appropriate Role will make you fearless.

Having a solid, clear Intention and an appropriate
Role will make you fearless.

The concept of Role comes from the entertainment industry. In every movie, theater, or television performance, an actor assumes a Role. When the Role is done well, the audience believes the actor *is* this character. The performer's mannerisms, gestures, language, and physical being are so convincing that the audience believes the actor is playing herself. However, unlike an actor whose character is dictated by a script, *you* select a Role that comes from the many Roles you already assume with colleagues, friends, and prospects.

Which one suits you best? First, consider your innate abilities and skills, as well as how you already approach things at work and in your personal life. Here's how you would select an effective Role using the example of a school fundraiser. Note: This list is not all-inclusive but highlights a select number of Roles.

- The **Mobilizer** or field general is in charge. She supervises teams while focusing on the financial goal. Everyone reports to her because she's a pro at overseeing the event, staying on budget, and holding the teams accountable, so that the campaign is successful. She allocates people and resources as needed.

- A **Motivator** enjoys recruiting others to participate and serve on committees. Motivators have a knack for persuading people to give more—whether it's time, auction items, or donations to the school. Motivators use the "push" and "pull" method to be successful. For example, a Motivator will drive benefactors to increase their donations by describing how the young people will benefit from the fundraiser (push), and the exposure they'll receive from participating (pull).

- A **Visionary** sees the big picture and is always looking ahead. She envisions the type of event that will serve the school's needs and what theme or experience will produce the best outcome.

- A **Coach** knows the players on her team—their strengths and weaknesses—and drives them to do their best. She's in the trenches, working alongside her team, and always has the end goal in sight.

- A **Liaison** knows where to get the best resources because she's functioned in that capacity for past events. Whether it's to vet and hire a caterer, or locate a printer, she will identify and make those connections.

- A **Facilitator** is well organized. She likes using her administrative skills to do tasks such as coordinating receipts and paperwork, following up with volunteers, and making sure things like invitations are sent on time. She works well behind the scenes, running meetings and efficiently handling the details.

When choosing a speaking Role, start with what you've already done and makes you comfortable. I often serve as **Liaison** within my network of professional service providers, connecting them to each other. The CEO of a charitable organization inspires volunteers when she selects the Role of **Visionary**. A sole practitioner takes on the Role of **Mobilizer** when she needs to convince a client that she can handle a large project. She speaks confidently about the personnel and physical resources she'll assemble and oversee.

When we work one-on-one with clients, our default Role is often the **Trusted Advisor.** (Please see the appendix for the Trusted Advisor Template©.) This is the only Role that incorporates both details and the big picture. For example, you're meeting with the human-resources director of a large real estate firm who's stressed about making payroll. Your Intention is to have her see you as a supportive partner. As an empathetic Trusted Advisor you could say, "It must be difficult to be the caretaker of your staff and having to let people go after a downturn in the economy."

You demonstrate your understanding of the situation by saying something like, "I remember when I ran my own production company. Whenever we had lean months, I worried about whether I could meet payroll or whether I'd have to let someone go." Or you share insights about the industry: "You're not the only one experiencing difficulty right now. Until the market absorbs all the short sales and foreclosures, there is too much inventory. And home prices are stagnant. Nearly all of my clients in real estate are facing tough times." As the client's Trusted Advisor, you'd ask thoughtful questions, be a good listener, and convey the right tone to let the human-resources director know that you're there for her.

If it's too soon or inappropriate to give advice, then the Trusted Advisor tells the story of another client in a similar position who managed to overcome her obstacles. But is a Trusted Advisor the best choice for public speaking? No. When you're in front of an audience, the empathic tone doesn't project well. A one-on-one connection is impossible. And it's simply not feasible to ask the right questions or address the needs of everyone in the audience.

On occasion, I'll hear a business consultant present her topic as a Trusted Advisor. This is the Role she's comfortable with and most likely assumes every day with her clients. But in front of a large audience, the Trusted Advisor's calm delivery falls flat. The problem isn't the content; it's that the speaker has chosen the wrong Role.

Which are the best Roles when speaking in public? Although there isn't one right answer, if I had to choose the most dynamic Role for engaging an audience, it would be the **Seasoned Veteran**.

If I had to choose the most dynamic Role for engaging an audience, it would be the Seasoned Veteran.

Once I hit fifty, I had fewer doubts about my abilities or what people thought of me. It's the same with Seasoned Veterans. They've won, they've lost, and they have the battle scars to prove it. Rather than giving advice, they'll tell you what they've learned. It's up to you whether you want to pay heed. Seasoned Veterans are comfortable looking back in time as well as forward. They make predictions based on their experience. And they count more on street smarts than book learning.

A Seasoned Veteran tells colorful stories and paints vivid pictures when she speaks. Most enjoy public speaking and know how to captivate an audience. They'll often use "If, then" statements: "If you do X and Y, then you'll get Z." Their sentences tend to be short and punchy. To them, hearing a long-winded explanation indicates that someone hasn't identified or can't articulate what's important. A Seasoned Veteran doesn't waste time, energy, or effort.

Another attribute of a Seasoned Veteran is her ability to project certainty and commitment. When I'm not feeling very confident, I'll put on the cloak of Seasoned Veteran and send *her* in. The Role gives me a boost and makes me feel less exposed.

When I'm training with David, I prefer to take on the Role of **Facilitator**. Starting and stopping Eloqui workshops on time, making sure everyone participates, and completing the agenda is my strong suit. During the actual training, I thoroughly enjoy uncovering the key message in someone's self-introduction or rearranging their content for maximum effect. Listening and giving them the tools for a "take two" is the most natural thing in the world for me.

What about you? What are your favorite Roles? Typically, we're better at one than another. But that doesn't mean we shouldn't stretch and move outside our comfort zone, especially if we want to advance in business, communicate effectively, and speak in public.

> *Teresa always saw herself as her father's daughter. She emulated everything about him, from his hairstyle to his wardrobe of dark suits. An executive in the insurance industry specializing in safety, Teresa provides policies to schools, manufacturing plants, and other places where workers could be injured on the job.*
>
> *Years ago, we conducted a workshop at Teresa's insurance firm. We called on her to explain what set her apart and why a school district or plant should do business with her company.*
>
> *Teresa gave a traditional and generic pitch, listing the features and benefits of the coverage. Her voice had little expression. She stumbled on occasion, but she fulfilled the assignment. However, since no one had any idea why providing safety policies and procedures was important to Teresa, it was easy to discount or reject what she said.*

When you sound like everyone else in your field, you risk being seen as a commodity. So when a prospective client doesn't understand what sets you apart or can't appreciate your unique value, the client will make a decision based on price.

Fortunately, Teresa was committed to implementing strong communication tools and came to our office for one-on-one coaching. She felt pressured by the high-stakes nature of these presentations, and would default to sounding like an expert—which wasn't getting her the results she wanted. I knew that changing her ingrained behavior wasn't going to be easy.

In a deceptively simple exercise, I asked Teresa to assume the attributes of a Role and tell me about safety, her area of expertise. I couldn't decide whether the Role of Motivator, Seasoned Veteran, or Facilitator would be best for her, so I assumed she'd use the one that resonated most with her.

I gave Teresa a number of possible Roles and asked her to deliver one to two minutes of content through the filter of each one. I told her I didn't care if her statistics and technical information were accurate, because that wasn't the purpose of the exercise. We started with Visionary and ended with Liaison. I was shocked. Teresa was a chameleon. With very little preparation, she easily assumed the language, behavior, and physical demeanor of each Role.

Going forward, the practical value to Teresa was that she could interview potential clients, assess what would most convince them, and speak through the filter of that particular Role. For example, she could be the Trusted Advisor or Coach when talking one-on-one with a client. When addressing an audience, she could send in the Motivator or Seasoned Veteran and not feel vulnerable or exposed. But the one Role I'd never let Teresa assume again was the **Technical Expert**, because it would not serve her Intention and would only increase her anxiety.

Teresa's main takeaway was that her job was not to educate her clients, but to convince them of the critical nature of having safety measures in place.

From that moment on, Teresa went beyond the assumption of Roles. In her next presentation, she held up her right hand. She shared the details of the factory accident where a machine cut off one of her fingers. After a pregnant pause, Teresa assured the audience that this accident never would have happened if her employer had put safety policies and procedures in place. She later relayed this moving example to us, saying, "Gets 'em every time!"

Three years later I received an email from Teresa. In addition to changing firms, she'd run for office as a national spokesperson for her industry. Teresa told us how much she now enjoys giving speeches and persuading her audience. Like many of our clients, she found that when she had permission to be herself and use her innate abilities, she had less anxiety and felt more confident and successful when speaking in public.

As speakers, we can borrow a page from the actor's playbook. There's a good reason why A-list performers study the *back story* of their character to fully inhabit a Role. They know what their character wants and why, even from a young age. This is how an actor transforms herself and is able to give a believable, credible, and memorable performance.

When you present, your Role also requires you to be congruent with your language and behavior. Think of how a director might describe the characteristics that define your Role. For example, a Mobilizer is strong and powerful, with erect posture and direct eye contact. A Visionary will typically speak in loftier rhetoric, and look off into the distance, literally and figuratively. The Facilitator is inclusive and solicits input from the audience, while keeping track of time for events such as breaks and meals. A Motivator exudes high energy and has no trouble telling her audience what they need to do to achieve the desired outcome.

When you present, your Role requires you to be congruent with your language and behavior.

As non-actors, we need direction. Once you're clear which Roles are aligned with your experience, take the next step. Is the purpose of your presentation to convey the big picture? If so, select a Role such as Seasoned Veteran, Motivator, Visionary, or Mobilizer. If your responsibility is to handle the process, details, or nuts and bolts, then choose the Role of Facilitator, Liaison, or Coach. Once you've taken on a definitive Role, the audience knows what to expect. You'll feel stronger and better equipped to persuade your listeners. After all, you're sending in that authoritative Role—not yourself.

A Role is also a great editing device. For example, a Coach doesn't need to give you a history of the sport for you to believe her recommendations and follow her fitness regimen. We don't expect our Coach to be a historian, writer, or scholar. We *do* expect her to know our individual abilities, have a workout routine for improving those abilities, and monitor the talents of the team for the most successful outcome.

Remember to combine Role and Intention. A speaker who doesn't correctly assess her audience in advance and chooses the wrong Role has to work much harder to succeed.

After you've decided on a Role, look for examples in your own life. Who do you know who is a Seasoned Veteran and how does that person show up? Who's a Motivator and how does she sound? Whom do you consider your Trusted Advisor and why do you have confidence in that person?

Then try on the Role and see how it feels. Did the Role allow you to achieve your desired outcome? Did it make you feel more at ease in front of the room? Keep rehearsing until you feel comfortable—this is how the process works.

We all start somewhere. I'm amazed when someone tells me that she's not good at public speaking. Anything of value that we've achieved takes time and experimentation. Speaking is no different. But when you journey outside your comfort zone, take risks, and applaud your success, there's no doubt that you will improve. And Roles are the best way to get there.

7

ENGAGE THE AUDIENCE FROM START TO FINISH

To anchor a talk in your audience's memory requires creativity in all three areas: your open, middle, and close. If you design these elements with care, your foundation is rock solid.

DIVE OFF A CLIFF

How you open your speech is critical to any presentation. I recommend you deliver a compelling opening and closing without the agenda slide, Power-Point, or video. This is where the audience gets to know *you*. Be selfish. Connect without standing behind a lectern or having anything that creates distance between you and your listeners. Openings set the hook, create the frame, and establish a connection with your audience. Done well, a good opening can reduce your anxiety during the rest of the presentation.

A speaker has only a brief window of time when the audience gives her the luxury of their full attention. During this honeymoon period of about thirty seconds, you can grab the audience or leave them cold. Like any marriage, this period determines whether the rest of your talk will be smooth sailing or you'll be clawing your way out of a bottomless pit.

But how do most speakers open? They copy one another, saying things like, "Good morning. My name is Deborah and over the next hour I'm going to cover . . ." Or, "I'd like to thank so-and-so for . . ." Audiences have heard these obligatory openings so often that they've lost all meaning. When you follow this old model, your listeners are likely to tune you out and tune into their smartphones.

Done well, a good opening can reduce your anxiety during the rest of the presentation.

Instead of giving a traditional welcome or delivering meaningless platitudes, use the moment to make your audience see you and your content in a new way. Remember how I opened the keynote to women business owners at the Reagan Library in Simi Valley, California? Following is an expanded version with the transition from skydiving to my topic.

> *The noise was deafening. The wind howled. Being the smallest, I was last in line. I scooted on my butt towards the giant gaping plane door.*
>
> *Finally, it was my turn. The flight master tapped me on the back. I let go of the struts and sank like a stone. But then I remembered to pull the cord. And when I looked up, I saw the most beautiful sight in the world—my red, blue, and yellow chute providing a canopy as I drifted toward Earth.*
>
> *For many of us, public speaking is just like jumping out of a plane. We feel terror, anxiety, and physical symptoms that we can't control, like shortness of breath or blanking out and being unable to think on our feet. There is a way to land safely and feel the exhilaration of conquering our fears. How can we, as women, find our authentic voice? That's what I'm going to discuss today.*

Paint a picture with your opening. Use the opportunity to hook your audience. Your listeners will be fully engaged when they can visualize your words.

Be specific when you share your perspective or experience with the topic, or describe something colorful that we wouldn't expect. For example, **Marilyn**, a divorce attorney, might open with, "In 2016, there has been an explosion in divorce among seniors. This new phenomenon is called grey divorce. Over the next forty-five minutes, I'll cover the unique needs of this growing population and how this crisis affects the entire family."

Eloqui has devised triggers to stimulate the imagination and give you choices to construct an opening. Don't be afraid to audition different triggers when you're preparing your talk so that each presentation will have a unique opening. Remember, audiences respond to variety, so you never want to be predictable.

When putting together your next presentation, or introduction of your services, pick one of the following and be creative.

- Find a strong metaphor or simile that gives your audience a vivid image of your business or topic.

- Compare a favorite movie, television show, or book to your topic. It can be the plot, characters, or theme.

- Recall a setback or disappointment that had a positive outcome and relate it to your talk.

- Identify a mentor who has had a major influence on you. How has this person affected your values or operating principles?

- Share one memorable sporting event or competition and the lessons learned that apply to your subject matter.

- Tell a story or anecdote that highlights the essence of your presentation or what type of business you want to attract.

Your default trigger can be to take a recent news item and link it to your topic. Great speakers throughout time have been immediate and present. When you reference a current event, the audience knows they're hearing fresh material that has been tailored to them.

> When you reference a current event, the audience knows they're hearing fresh material that has been tailored to them.

Here's how President Barack Obama opened the dedication to the 9/11 Memorial. Notice his use of concrete language, visual snapshots, and theme.

In those awful moments after the South Tower was hit, some of the injured huddled in the wreckage of the 78th floor. The fires were spreading. The air was filled with smoke. It was dark, and they could barely see. It seemed as if there was no way out.

And then there came a voice—clear, calm, saying he had found the stairs. A young man in his 20s, strong, emerged from the smoke and over his nose and his mouth he wore a red handkerchief.

They didn't know his name. They didn't know where he came from. But they knew their lives had been saved by the man in the red bandana . . .[91]

The president gave his obligatory thanks after those opening remarks that mesmerized the audience. When you have individuals or companies to acknowledge, put these remarks *after* your opening.

Once you've delivered your colorful opening, make an intelligent link to your topic. One common mistake is to begin with such a vivid and lengthy opening that it becomes the focus of your presentation or self-introduction—rather than a lead-in to introduce your topic or services.

__Betsy__ needed to establish credibility with potential customers but was hesitant to stray from her bank's standard pitch.

After digging into Betsy's past, I extracted this childhood story for her self-introduction: "Banking is in my blood. My father was the president of a bank, and every year before Christmas, my gifts were stored in the vault so I couldn't find them. I've always viewed banks as the place where good things are secured and protected." If Betsy were talking to a client, or speaking at a conference, she could add, "So today I will be describing how our bank's services protect your assets."

Once you've delivered your colorful opening, make an intelligent link to your topic.

Openings can also be effective in setting the tone for an entire event. One executive came to us after being hired by a large company.

__Roberta__ had the task of hosting a two-day conference for service providers in the California State University system. Because she knew so little about the attendees, she was anxious about crafting her introductory remarks.

Together, we constructed the following: "My mother raised me as a single parent in upstate New York. Our town was so small that our phone number was 17. I've met more people at this company over the last three days than I met in the first nine years of my life."

Roberta's opening effectively warmed up the audience and let them know she was looking forward to meeting each and every one of them over the next few weeks. Not surprisingly, the rest of her hosting responsibilities went smoothly.

VARIATIONS ON A THEME

Use your opening to suggest a theme, which is an easily repeated phrase or sentence. Themes can be revisited in various ways throughout your presentation. Themes are not a one-word concept, like dreams, success, or retirement. A theme is the core idea summed up in a simple phrase or sentence.

A theme is the core idea summed up in a simple phrase or sentence.

Memorable themes from our professional clients include "The language of retirement," "Trust no one," and "Gift your children, not the IRS." Themes allow an audience to understand technical information. They provide context and an effective way to frame difficult concepts. And themes affect pacing and momentum, driving a talk forward. Notice the theme in the following opening.

Working at my last company was like playing musical chairs. One day the music stopped and I was laid off. My chair was yanked out from under me. At the next company, my chair was a bit wobbly, but I made it work.

To keep the audience engaged, this engineer revisited her theme of "playing musical chairs" throughout her presentation.

Speaker anxiety plagues amateurs and professionals alike. As mentioned earlier, anxiety tends to spike just before and in the first few minutes of any presentation. The best way to reduce speaker anxiety is to open with something that happened to you or that you know well. When you deliver a personal anecdote or share your take on a subject, you will have no fear of being found out. And, by exhibiting personal charm and self-effacing humor instead of telling a joke, we are not asking the audience to laugh or find us funny. Remember the line by actor Edmund Gwenn: "Dying is easy. Comedy is hard."[92]

A few years ago, I coached **Rita**, an attorney who was asked to thank sponsors and volunteers at a charity event. Despite being an accomplished litigator, she kept forgetting her prepared remarks.

After her coaching session, I determined that Rita's forgetfulness had nothing to do with her intellectual ability or her passion for the charity. She couldn't remember her remarks because they didn't mean anything to her. I encouraged Rita to speak from her own experience and make her acknowledgments relevant.

I've paraphrased what she delivered. "I love to shop. When I was eighteen, my sister Angie and I could cover as many as five malls a day. I'm fortunate to still have my sister Angie. A few years ago, she developed cancer, and if it weren't for the efforts of people like you, I would have lost her. (Rita placed her obligatory thanks here.) But there's a silent auction going on next door, and I hate to miss any opportunity to shop, so please join me!"

Rita had no trouble remembering these remarks and received high praise for her unique and personal approach.

Have your opening down cold. Since the opening sets the tone and the frame for everything that follows, don't wing it. Like an A-list performer, have a clear idea of what you'll say. Then rearrange the phrases or modify the wording and phrasing each time you rehearse it so you'll sound natural and spontaneous. The other benefit in rehearsing your opening in different ways (as opposed to memorizing) is that it will be authentic and engaging however it's conveyed.

The first time you construct a colorful opening, it may have too many elements or may be too long. That's OK. This is the construction phase. Have fun and play with the various possibilities, then exercise your critical acumen to shorten it up or find even more colorful terms to incorporate the second time.

Capturing the audience's attention with your opening remarks feels wonderful. And that energy will propel you forward.

DON'T GO SOFT IN THE MIDDLE

Once you have a compelling opening, you've effectively set the stage for what comes next. The middle of the presentation is where the bulk of your content resides. This is also the section where you can be the most persuasive.

Your opening is emotional, tapping into the right side of the brain. Once you introduce your concept, you have the entire middle section to provide evidence to support it. The most effective way to deliver this content is to organize it in such a way that you and the audience can process and remember it.

To begin, I draw three boxes on a piece of paper or a tablet. Then I assign a title to each one. I divide up my content and place it into one of these three buckets or under these headings.

Let's reference Marilyn again, the attorney who specializes in divorce for older adults who are splitting up after being married for a long time.

When she speaks on the topic, her Intention is to be seen as the go-to person in grey divorce, which is surging in the United States. She has chosen the Role of Seasoned Veteran, because she doesn't want to educate the audience so much that they decide they can handle a divorce themselves or use a service they found online. She also doesn't want to overload the audience with too many technical details.

Marilyn separates her content into the following talking points or buckets:

1. How to prepare if you're considering divorce;
2. What you'll face during the divorce process;
3. What life looks like after the divorce is final.

Once Marilyn has categorized her material, she has a better idea of what to leave in, and more important, what to take out. We all know a lot about our topic, but the audience doesn't need to know or care about everything.

To accomplish her Intention, Marilyn shares well-crafted stories in which she's the hero. She demonstrates her knowledge of current regulations and includes her opinion with "I" statements about how she works within the system. She also customizes her content to suit the audience, so each listener feels that Marilyn understands her unique situation and circumstances.

Clear delineation means Marilyn can now determine how best to present her material—everything from incorporating examples of how she served her divorcing clients and provided critical financial advice, to leading audience breakout exercises with a partner. Rather than presenting the material in each bucket the same way, Marilyn changes it up whenever she gives this presentation. She also looks for ways to get the audience actively involved. Two of the best ways to engage an audience are variety and creativity.

The other consideration when structuring the middle of your presentation is to cover everything in each bucket before transitioning to the next one. Note: Movement can telegraph a change in content. Before starting the next bucket, walk to another part of the stage or space with a transitional line that indicates you are beginning a new section. Do whatever you can to separate the ideas and concepts for the audience.

FINISH STRONG

If the opening sets the tone and frame, the close is what the audience remembers most. Instead of racing to finish, letting your voice trail off, or asking for questions, stay focused on engaging your audience through the very last word.

There are many different ways to close your presentation. Always consider your Intention and then make the best guess as to which closing device to employ. There is no one right way.

For any close, use short phrases and sentences. Pause between each one. If you're going to give a list of items, three is the ideal number. Remember to slow down—a bit of dramatic emphasis works well with closing remarks. To keep you and your audience engaged, select a different close for each presentation you give on the same topic.

Seven Eloqui Closing Techniques

1. **Inspirational quotes**

   Quotes can come from someone notable in history (but preferably long dead and not political). Or you can make one up, giving credit to a family member or colleague. One great online source is quotationspage.com.

2. **Recap**

   Pick three main points from your presentation. Think of this closing device as your highlight reel. Don't telegraph by saying, "In summary" or "As I said" or "To recap." Simply pause and then list the three things you want the audience to remember.

For example, the recap for a talk on communication skills could be, "To make your talk memorable, incorporate visual snapshots, great stories, novelty, and surprise. Always be yourself. Authenticity gives you credibility."

3. Established theme

Revisit your established theme. Typically the idea for a theme, or easily repeated phrase, is suggested in your opening remarks. Effective themes describe the whole idea of your presentation. For the close, you can be creative about various ways to fold it in—themes can go in the beginning, middle, or final sentence of your close.

4. Call to action

A strong call to action uses active and punchy verbs. When concluding an Eloqui workshop, we might say the following: "Don't stop improving your communication skills. When you leave here today, incorporate one new skill at a time until it becomes part of your muscle memory. Put as much attention on your delivery as you do your content. And when you commit to becoming an engaging speaker, audiences will listen."

A strong call to action uses active and punchy verbs.

5. Repetition in triplicate form

Begin each of three statements with the same phrase, such as "I believe . . ." or "I know . . ." or "Together we can . . ."

List these three statements in ascending order of importance. For example: "I believe anyone can become a great speaker . . . I believe when you incorporate visual snapshots, novelty and surprise, and authenticity, you're well on your way . . . And, I believe that if everyone spoke this way, I'd never be bored at another business presentation!"

Don't say anything after the third statement or start a new section. This technique is a curtain closer and extremely effective on a large stage, but can also be used to close a one-on-one pitch. Think of it as selling without selling. For example: "No matter whom you use for your communication-skills training, make sure they are field-trained, make sure they listen and respond to your needs, and make sure they customize the program to you."

6. **Personal anecdote or case study**

You can end your presentation with an example just as easily as you can begin with one. If your material has been technical or high level, consider a story for your close.

7. **Bookend your opening**

In this close, come back to how you opened your presentation, but add one new insight. You can employ this technique anytime you need to cut short a presentation, pitch, or negotiation. When a speaker bookends her talk, the audience has a sense of coming full circle. There's resolution and completion.

The Bookend is my default close. I always know how I opened, so the material is easy to access. There are colorful details I can incorporate. And if the decision maker says, "Sorry, Deborah, I said you had forty-five minutes, but I have to take this conference call. Can you wrap it up, please?" I don't rush. I deliver my most important point and then close with the Bookend.

For my speech at the Reagan Library, here's how I closed: "For about a week after jumping out of a plane and landing safely, I felt invincible. I drove twenty miles over the speed limit. I said whatever was on my mind. And I was energized. That's my wish for you. Jump out of a plane and speak in public. Feel the exhilaration of connecting with the audience. When people tell you they liked what you had to say, let their comments sink in . . . Thank you."

Performers know the close is the time to commit, invest themselves in their material, and make it more important to them, not the audience. Do the same with your presentations. Pause before launching your close. Make eye contact around the room. Slow down. Keep your sentences short. With total confidence and full energy, you'll "bring the curtain down."

8

MOVE WITH PURPOSE

Movement onstage is physical grammar. Done well and with purpose, movement can underline the importance of a statement, allow the audience to track with your content, or delineate transitions between topics. Movement keeps the speaker energized and in control of her space.

Once you've identified your Intention and Role, spend some time thinking about your physical gestures and movement—everything should match. When speakers move as soon as they walk on stage, it's because they need to bleed off energy, they're feeling anxious, or they think that they're supposed to. The problem is that humans are mammals, so our eyes follow or track any kind of movement. Movement is a powerful tool; it should be used sparingly. It also needs to be justified and should complement your words. How can we focus on your message if you never hold still?

For your open and close, don't move. Instead, stand in the center of the space. Make a connection with your audience and let them get acquainted with you. Gesture with your hands, and be flexible from the waist up, but save movement for when you need to emphasize a point *after* your opening.

Start with your arms and hands hanging loosely at your sides, rather than folded, stuck in pockets, or hiding your private parts. It may feel awkward to have your arms at your sides, but within seconds you'll gesture to make a point. No matter what anyone has told you, there's no such thing as being "too expressive." We all gesture in private conversations to make a point. This technique will allow you to act naturally when you're on a bigger stage.

For your open and close, don't move. Instead, stand in the center of the space and gesture naturally.

Once you're into the main portion of your talk, there are appropriate moves to support your content. For example, if you want to emphasize a comment, cross downstage on an angle toward your audience. Moving on an angle indicates importance or a critical nature, without your having to say, "This is important." The move serves as an exclamation point. Tailor it to the size of the stage. In a small space, one to two steps is sufficient. On a larger stage, take three or four steps.

However, once you've made the cross downstage, stay in that spot to deliver the next few lines. If you immediately back up, you're telegraphing that you don't really believe the important point you just made.

Often clients say, "If I want to make an important point, why not move directly toward the audience?" This move is too aggressive. However, if you want to share a secret or an aside, walk directly toward the audience and lower your voice. You'll notice people leaning in to hear you. Bingo. You've got them right where you want them.

To return upstage, or away from the audience, you can simply back up, especially if you've marked out the space and know where the back wall is. Or, you can maintain eye contact with your audience while you form a button-hook, walking in a semi-circle upstage. Begin with your upstage leg and practice so that your return doesn't look awkward or stilted.

Let's say you have a number of items to present or you want the audience to consider multiple points. To deliver a list, walk back and forth in a straight line, on a parallel plane with your audience. It's up to you to decide where to stop, but maintain eye contact with the audience while you talk. College professors often use this technique while teaching.

If you have two separate topics or sections, feel free to mark out two distinct areas of the stage. Finish speaking about one topic in one space, and then walk to another part of the stage for the second. It doesn't matter where the two spots are. It only matters that you've defined them for the audience.

There's a move that should be employed only *once* during a presentation. Finish your statement. Turn and walk upstage with your back to the audience. Don't speak while you walk. Then turn to face the audience. Whatever you say next should have a big impact. This works because speakers don't typically turn their backs on an audience. So when you do this, they'll pay attention. Consider it a bit of theatrical punctuation.

Warning: It's harder than you think to walk and talk at the same time. When a speaker raises the toes of her foot or leans forward on an angle, she's telegraphing an upcoming move. Or she's being tentative. The same is true if a speaker moves on an angle and then doesn't plant both feet. Always check to see that you've completed the move. It takes a bit of practice.

If you're delivering your presentation sitting at a table, many of these same moves apply. Angle your body in either direction when you want to make an important point. Lean in to listen more intently to whoever is speaking. Back your chair away from the table if you want to give yourself more real estate and set up a more dramatic move. Make eye contact with everyone in the room—not just the decision maker. Gesture naturally, rather than restricting your hands or keeping them in your lap.

Movement may sound complicated, but don't be overly concerned about doing it right. Remember that less is more. Start by incorporating one movement at a time. During your next presentation, try walking back and forth as you deliver a list. Or walk directly toward the audience, lower your voice, and share a secret or aside. Maybe you want to try moving out from behind the lectern to present in the middle of the stage, with nothing between you and the audience.

Just remember to be yourself. That's more important than movement. Some speakers will never be comfortable moving, while others enjoy movement because it gives them the freedom to be more than a talking head.

Even if you don't move, gesture to give your voice a more musical quality, to breathe and allow oxygen to fill your lungs, and to appear confident and comfortable. Stand firm to support that out-of-body feeling that may come over you. And know that from the moment you move out front, you own the room.

COMMON THEATER TERMS
AND MOVEMENT TECHNIQUES

Downstage: Moving toward the audience and away from the back wall.

Justified movement: Moving with a purpose; e.g., on an angle to make an emphatic point, directly toward the audience to share an aside or secret, or returning to the center of the space to revisit the established theme. This is the opposite of wandering aimlessly or moving for the sole purpose of expelling nervous energy.

Lateral movement: Walking back and forth on a parallel plane to the audience, signifying "I'm thinking," "Consider these points," or "Here is a list . . ."

Most powerful movement: Crossing at an angle toward the audience to make an important point from upstage to downstage. The speaker is breaking two planes—horizontal as well as vertical. The angle should be no greater than forty-five degrees and proportionate to the size of the space.

Physical grammar: Utilizing movement for emphasis. Examples: creating an exclamation point by moving on an angle toward the audience; using commas to deliver a list while walking back and forth on a parallel plane with the audience; or stopping anywhere on the stage to signify a period.

Pulling focus: Drawing audience attention during a group presentation through physical gestures, movement, or eye contact. This behavior is distracting and unprofessional.

Redefining center: An alternative to returning repeatedly to the middle of the space. Speakers can move from behind a lectern or choose another spot as center stage, as long as they physically stay open to the entire room.

Repetitive gesture: A noticeable movement that repeats and is distracting to the audience, like counting on one's fingers, putting on and removing glasses, or finger pointing.

Shrink the room: Drawing the audience in by lowering one's voice and delivering an aside or secret, while directly approaching the audience. Doing this makes the room feel smaller and more intimate.

Stage directions: Always defined from the speaker's point of view. For example, crossing downstage left would mean the speaker moves left on a diagonal toward the audience.

Upstage: Moving away from the audience and toward the back wall.

Vis-à-vis: When two speakers stand next to one another on the same plane. The correct distance for two presenters is an arm's length apart, and turned slightly to one's partner. This positioning enables the pair to stay open to the audience, while keeping each other in clear view.

9

TECHNOLOGY— FRIEND OR FOE?

Presentation software like PowerPoint can overshadow a presenter. Use it only when absolutely necessary. To avoid being upstaged by PowerPoint, don't go onstage or into a pitch without techniques to keep you front and center.

The best application of PowerPoint or alternative programs is visual aids, or to show relationships. However, most presenters depend on it as a crutch or cueing device. They place their content or script on the screen, and read it. If that's their approach, why do we need them?

PowerPoint is the unruly gorilla in the room, but there are any number of similar software applications, including Prezi, Keynote, Haiku Deck, Slide-Rocket, and at least twenty-five others. Before you use any of these platforms, ask yourself: Do I really need a slide deck? Does this client or industry demand it? Is PowerPoint appropriate to the size of the venue and number of viewers? If your answer is no, then don't use it. I've seen many presenters upstaged by PowerPoint.

I admit, sometimes you can't avoid using a few PowerPoint slides, especially when it's expected by your audience or you're one of the rare folks who actually like it. If that's the case, make sure you use the technology properly.

First rule of thumb: Don't use PowerPoint for your open or close. You want the audience to focus on you and your message. When I see the presenter's first slide detailing her agenda, I look for the exits because more likely than not, the presentation is going to be predictable, lengthy, and boring.

Traditionally, speakers designed their presentations by following the Power-Point AutoContent Wizard and filling in information. Then templates were developed, which weren't any more creative. Resist the temptation to use them. This chronological, linear way of constructing material diminishes the effectiveness of the speaker and limits options.

It's possible (but rare) for PowerPoint to be effective and enhance a presentation. I give high grades to PowerPoint decks that incorporate graphs, charts, photos, animation, and brief videos. When your presentation is visual or shows the relationship between items or concepts, the audience readily absorbs your content. But even though the material is presented on a large screen, *you* still need to be in control. There are ways PowerPoint can be the creative medium it was designed to be.

> ## There are ways PowerPoint can be the creative medium it was designed to be.

Make your slides visual and brief. Marilyn—the attorney who's pitching new clients—can use an organizational chart to showcase all the players in a divorce, including family members, attorneys, financial advisors, accountants, and real estate professionals. This graphic quickly allows the audience to see who's involved. Marilyn can then relate how she interacts with each of the players and what their services typically cost.

To begin each section, verbally provide your listeners with an overview to orient them. It could be an example, a question, or, for Marilyn, a declarative statement like, "Going through a divorce may feel like a dark tunnel that stretches on forever. But there is light at the end of that tunnel, and I guarantee you will come out the other side."

You have a very specific job with this medium—to be the translator or interpreter. No slide should stand on its own without your telling us what we need to know. If you're simply reciting the words on each slide, then eventually the audience will ignore you.

Look through your deck and figure out one key takeaway per slide. This process will also let you know when you have too much content on any one slide, or you need to divide it into multiple slides. You can also eliminate the sub-bullets, or build the list so that each item comes up one at a time. When you have a lot of content on one slide, you can highlight, bold, or put key phrases in another color so that the audience can scan your slides and return their attention to you. Be economical. But do whatever it takes to keep the focus on you and your interpretation of the content.

Look through your deck and figure out one key takeaway per slide.

Whether you're a retail analyst presenting buying data, or an insurance professional speaking on new health-care laws, it's difficult not to let the material lead. You have a dilemma when tasked with delivering technical information. Whenever *all* of the information is up on the screen, it can easily overwhelm both the speaker and the audience.

Use variety and change it up. Write on a whiteboard or flip chart—anything to keep your audience from being put to sleep by the PowerPoint. Instead of reading the bullet points from top to bottom, go out of order. You can say, "All of these features are important, but my favorite is number three because everything else hinges on the success of social media." Make the audience know that you are the main act and the one to listen to. Beyoncé has backup singers, but they're never as beautiful, as talented, or costumed quite as well as QueenB. She's a pro.

If you can, position yourself vis-à-vis and an arm's length from the screen, so it's like your partner. If you're downstage from the screen (toward the audience), you are upstaging yourself whenever you look back at the screen and away from the audience.

Use a high-quality remote, such as the Logitech Wireless Presenter R400. It's small, and can be palmed so the audience doesn't see it and you can still gesture naturally. My favorite button on this model is the black-box icon, which is the same as the "b" button on your keyboard. When you hit the icon or "b" button, the screen goes black and you can tell a story, connect with the audience, or move in front of the screen. When you hit the button again, you return to the slide you were on and can keep advancing.

TALE OF TWO DECKS

I highly recommend constructing a presenter's deck and a leave-behind deck. The presenter's deck is a lean, visual PowerPoint that supports your verbal presentation. The leave-behind deck has more data and is designed to be read and reviewed carefully at a later time. You can give the richer version to whoever requests it, but to keep people's attention, I recommend you pass it out *after* the audience has heard you. To simplify your life and shorten your prep time, begin by constructing the leave-behind deck. Then remove sub-bullets and anything else you'll be addressing in your talk. What's left is your presenter's deck.

I highly recommend constructing a presenter's deck and a leave-behind deck.

WHAT CAN GO WRONG WILL GO WRONG

Any and all technology can and will fail, so be sure to rehearse, and take backups of batteries, flash drives, connecting cables, and anything you can think of that might malfunction. Most important, rehearse without any tech; just in case everything fails, you will be fine. If this happens, laugh it off. Give a simple apology and make the best of it. Presenters who carry on in spite of tech failure show resolve, and engineer the impression they will be reliable partners.

Microphone Dos and Don'ts

This technology still creates problems in the modern age. Many speakers, particularly presenters on award shows and executives at charity functions, lean in too close to a microphone and "P-pop," or blast the audience with every P, B, T, K, or F.

Position any fixed or handheld microphone about three inches from you and point it at your chin, not your mouth. Speak slightly over the mic, so your voice sounds good and you don't "P-pop." With lavaliere mics, clip them near the upper part of your lapel or blouse so you can be heard. Turn with your whole body, so you don't turn your head away from the mic and go silent when you look right or left. Don't tap your chest and mic when referring to yourself. And please don't fuss with your blouse or lapel. When you hit your mic, it will cause a scraping or scratching sound, which is distracting.

YOUR OWN ADVANCE TEAM

If possible, find out what technology will be available on site, whether it's a Mac or Windows operating system. You want to be sure your flash drive or device carrying your PowerPoint is compatible with whatever system is being used at the venue. Bring your own extension cords and power strips.

WHEN YOU'RE ON AN AUDIO OR VIDEO CONFERENCE CALL

New communication technology has dramatically cut back on travel expense. With webcam technologies like Google Hangouts, Skype, FaceTime, and Zoom Video Conferencing, we can virtually connect with colleagues or prospective clients around the world. Conference calls let us hear one another from many locations, and webinars supply a training tool. However, these applications have their limitations. Each one requires specific techniques to be effective.

Audio Conference Calls

Master the correct pronunciation of everyone's name. Make a list so you can visualize the attendees. Stand to keep your energy up. Don't look at anything else, like a computer or cell phone, unless you absolutely have to. Keep your focus on the others, as you would in normal conversation. This goes for any type of conference or call.

Videoconference Calls

When using a platform such as Skype, FaceTime, or Zoom, consider what your audience sees when you're on camera. Arrange a background that is simple and promotes your brand or service. Utilize lighting to look your best. Carefully select your wardrobe and keep it simple. Wear solid colors, defaulting to blue, which is best on camera. Avoid flashy jewelry or patterns—anything that distracts from your face.

Focus on the camera lens, not on others on the screen. If you do, you could be focused slightly below your audience. Speak as though everyone is right in front of you, with the conversational quality you have in a one-on-one meeting. Gesture as you would normally to give you energy so that you appear natural.

Speak as though everyone is right in front of you, with the conversational quality you have in a one-on-one meeting.

10

SERVE AND VOLLEY: COMMUNICATION AS A CONTACT SPORT

"I once talked a guy out of blowing up the Sears Tower, but I can't talk my wife out of the bathroom, or my kid off the phone."
—Kevin Spacey in *The Negotiator*

I love this quotation. I consider myself a communication specialist, and yet my partner David and I fight like angry first-graders. We know we're not supposed to pick at old wounds, reference how we were raised, or use words like "always" or "never"—but we do it anyway. If I'm really upset and believe he hasn't heard me, I'll ask him to *PLEASE* repeat back what I've said in his own words. Even though this is a technique we train in our seminars, David still refuses to do it. (My guess is he feels manipulated, but at that moment I really don't care.) Intellectually, we both know heightened emotions can cause even the most rational individual to go for the jugular.

I'm not a therapist, and wouldn't claim to be nonjudgmental or always considerate of my partner. But I am willing to share the tools, techniques, and safety nets I've gleaned from our clients, as well as my own experience, for defusing a situation when emotions run high and a lot is riding on the outcome. And *especially* when the heat is on, we need an assortment of techniques, in case one doesn't work or isn't enough.

My editor at BenBella Books, Amy Debra Feldman, recommended I devote an entire chapter to communication. She was right. Most of us participate in conversations a lot more often than we ever engage in public speaking—whether it's persuading our supervisor to buy into our project; managing client expectations; convincing our children that they should take responsibility for their actions; or defending our position when we have a cause we believe in. What I've also found from coaching women across all industries is that some of us experience more anxiety presenting to strangers, while others get more nervous presenting to our peers. Whichever is true for you, there are communication techniques to bolster you when you face down your demons—real or imagined.

We need to be flexible and nimble to master the art of communicating. Consider the words of German military strategist Helmuth von Moltke: "No battle plan survives contact with the enemy."[93] With public speaking, *you* control the pace and the message. With communication, at least one other person is involved—so the conversation must be fluid and include back-and-forth dialogue so others get a turn to speak.

Let's say you're pitching to a new client, customer, or buyer. You want to make sure the prospective client knows what you bring to the table and why your experience is exactly what's needed. In your mind, controlling the flow of the presentation is critical to your success. However, being in the flow also means allowing the recipient into the conversation. We've heard from pitch teams that they couldn't deliver their presentation as rehearsed because the client kept interrupting them.

I have to laugh. If the client starts to talk, stop immediately. Yield the floor so she can voice her concerns, questions, or clarifications. When the client is engaged in the conversation, you have a greater likelihood of success. While she is speaking, make a quick note of where you were in your presentation. You can always pick up where you left off and regain the momentum. However, if the client steers the presentation in another direction, be confident that you're still moving toward your goal. (The only exception is when a client spends too much time on a point that isn't germane to the discussion. Then you'll have to politely steer the conversation or pitch back on point. You can always say that you're happy to revisit that concern at a specific later time.) The ebb and flow between prepared presentation and conversational interaction is a dance. Being nimble and flexible always trumps being polished and precise.

The ebb and flow between prepared presentation and conversational interaction is a dance.

Another unique quality of communication is that it varies according to our culture, background, and personal relationships. My sister, Marci, and I finish each other's sentences. We've done it all our lives. We know each other so well, this is our shorthand.

However, our way of communicating frustrates our husbands. More than once I've heard David say, "How can you possibly know what the other is thinking?" or "That's incredibly rude." So when Marci and I are talking, rather than try to follow our conversation, he'll leave the room. I've stopped trying to explain that this is our version of familiarity and affection.

But I also know that if I finish his sentences (don't wives typically know what their husbands are going to say?) or interrupt him, I'm in trouble. David is southern, and was raised being polite and letting people finish their thoughts.

Depending on our age, we see the world differently. David and I developed a primer to bridge the divide between generations we labeled *youth* and *sage*. Here's what we suggest to facilitate communication between them.

Youth: Don't audition or tap dance because you feel fear or lack confidence. If you fall into that trap, you'll tend to say too much, stray off point, pontificate to show how much you know, and lose the attention of your client, customer, or audience.

Don't assume the more seasoned professional is ignorant of new technology. Show respect. Be curious. Demonstrate that you admire his or her knowledge and experience by asking questions. Take advantage of a more experienced person's willingness to mentor you. Her support is a fast track to gaining trust and deepening a potentially important relationship.

Sage: Express genuine interest in the younger professional and her expertise, especially when it comes to social media, apps, or Internet sites. Don't use a condescending tone. Make every meeting or connection an exercise in discovery.

Make every meeting or connection an exercise in discovery.

There are a few other generational differences we've observed. Typically, clients over forty tend to study written materials in depth, make notes, and adapt the research to their communication style. They struggle with deeply ingrained habits as well as a tendency to follow a rigid structure, which decreases spontaneity.

Younger clients tend to scan written materials and spend less time doing critical analysis, so their presentations can sound "light." On a positive note, they tend to make a quicker audience connection and convey a sense of immediacy. Clearly, their presentations aren't canned.

We believe the two demographic groups can learn from one another; that is, in-depth study and analysis produces gravitas and trust, while immediacy and conversational style produces confidence and likability.

TEN TIPS FOR SUCCESS

Tip #1: Go In with a Clear Intention of What You Want to Achieve

Figure out your purpose before you start the conversation or meeting. Having an Intention will keep you on track when the discussion goes sideways, there are distractions, or emotions run high. Examples of strong Intentions include: "I'll persuade them to fund my project," "They'll see me as the go-to attorney for mediating their divorce," "I'll that prove my IRS experience is critical to keeping them out of trouble."

In truth, many of the same Intentions will work for public speaking as well as one-on-one communications, but the strategy, execution, and tactics are different. In either case, it's critical to make sure your Intention fits the situation and the audience.

Have no more than three items or talking points that support your Intention, and prioritize them. On occasion, when circumstances change, or you receive push-back, you'll need to revise your Intention. This is rare, but if it happens, consider your options. You can shift your focus or double down on your commitment by delivering a different story or asking more questions to assess and answer the client's real concern.

Margaret *is an experienced appellate-court attorney who had an interview to become a court commissioner. Because she is statuesque, experienced, and articulate, you would think this would be a slam dunk—but not to Margaret. She felt as if she were facing a firing squad rather than answering questions from a panel of judges. A colleague and advocate told Margaret that the panel was concerned about her long-winded responses from an earlier interview; and more specifically, whether or not she could respond quickly in the job—as opposed to the thoughtful, lengthy process she practiced as an appellate-court attorney.*

Margaret came to us for coaching. First, we had to move her away from replaying what she perceived as mistakes in the earlier interview. Then we had to quiet the voices in her head that insisted she answer each question perfectly—which is impossible when you don't know what will be asked of you. An Analyzer who prided herself on giving thoughtful responses, Margaret needed a brief, actionable Intention.

Together we decided that the best Intention for her was, "I'll qualify to see if the fit is right." Hopefully, this Intention would take some of the pressure off her. Instead of the interview being a one-way street, it would be congruent with her Intention to ask the panel members some questions. Rather than auditioning, which can result in talking too much or sounding desperate, Margaret could relate what she enjoys about the law and how her extensive experience would allow her to make quick decisions when necessary.

We also rehearsed Margaret's three talking points and encouraged her to drop them into the conversation. Whether you're interviewing for a job or you've written a book and are answering media questions, it's up to you to highlight your strengths. For Margaret, that meant emphasizing her ability to make decisions based on the research she'd already done, to communicate with any type of audience because of the scope of cases she'd tried, and to serve as a utility player because of her non-profit work and membership in other legal associations.

Margaret emailed us after the interview. Note how hard she still is on herself, but hopefully that will change going forward. We need more women like Margaret taking center stage, out front:

"I felt confident but not perfect . . . I was escorted upstairs and 12 judges were sitting in a room . . . I would say I got a B— to B+ on content. I slipped up when they asked me what area of law I was passionate about. I said I wasn't really

passionate—but recovered by saying that I am passionate about a lot of things, but when it comes to the law, I am pretty adaptable . . . The judge who gave me the hardest time asked me about a project I worked on that is buried in my résumé.

"When I was escorted out, the same judge said it was a tough room, and I did fine. I told her that I argued before the Ninth Circuit and it was a breeze compared to this. I might have been off on content, but I was not nervous and did not falter in my Role as Seasoned Veteran. I got a nice boost when another judge said I came highly recommended for the position . . . It really does not matter if I get the position. It matters that I actually walked away feeling good about the process."

Before any meeting, interview, or pitch, determine your Intention. What's the outcome that you want to achieve? In your conversation, include only the material that supports your Intention (unless, like Margaret, you're instructed to answer a question in another area). Keep your comments brief and targeted. When you pare down your statements to what drives your Intention, and package them to move your audience of one or a hundred, you'll greatly increase your chances for success.

But what if your anxiety ramps up because a lot is riding on the outcome? Even with a solid Intention, the critical voices in your head can make communicating difficult, if not impossible. Then do what every shy actor does and take on a Role. Whether it's Seasoned Veteran, Motivator, or Trusted Advisor, you won't feel nearly as exposed and vulnerable (see chapter six, "The Value of Using Strong Technique," for complete descriptions of these and other Roles).

Whether you're interviewing for a job or you've written a book and are answering media questions, it's up to *you* to highlight your strengths.

Tip #2: Tell a Brief Story or Give "I" Statements

The best way to solidify your Intention, reduce your anxiety, and let others see your commitment is to include your experience. Too many of us were taught to leave ourselves out of the conversation, so we believe that talking about ourselves is self-aggrandizing, egotistical, or off-putting. The opposite is true. Unless the person sitting across from you knows why your idea, project, or service is important, you'll never convince her to change her mind. But when you share *your* story, the sky's the limit.

Unless the person sitting across from you knows why your idea, project, or service is important, you'll never convince her to change her mind.

Lucy came to us after she'd agreed to work in the development department of a Los Angeles hospital. In her new position, she was tasked with raising money for the facility to purchase a new type of mammogram machine to screen for breast cancer.

While working for another nonprofit, Lucy had successfully raised $50,000. Now she and her team were responsible for ten times that amount—per machine. In addition, although Lucy was comfortable working behind the scenes, she intensely disliked being in front of more than two people at a time. Although this hadn't been a problem in her previous career as an interior decorator, she needed to overcome her fear of being in the spotlight.

I asked Lucy why she was passionate about this project. She told me that, owing to having "lumpy" breast tissue, she often required multiple mammograms to make sure that she didn't have breast cancer. Lucy went in every year for these tests because she had a family history of the disease. The new machines were more sensitive and accurate, and required fewer annual visits. I encouraged Lucy to lead off with her story, which would not only reduce her anxiety, but also inspire and motivate her team. Her audience might disagree with her statistics, percentages, and technical details, but no one could question Lucy's commitment to bringing this new technology to the hospital.

She emailed me after her kickoff meeting. "A big *THANK YOU* for shelving my nerves. There were about 30 people in the room. I felt great and had zero anxiety. I even remembered everything I wanted to say. :)"

My favorite part was what Lucy heard from the senior development officer who'd recruited her to work on this project. (Note: The capitalizations are hers, not mine.) "*CONGRATULATIONS* on a successful meeting last night. You are *amazing! So articulate, so truthful and convincing. Your words and leadership inspired everyone!! You will be incredible in this role!! There is no doubt about it."*

Whether Lucy is pitching wealthy donors or motivating her team to increase its "ask," telling her story will make all the difference. So the next time a prospective client or employer wonders, "Why you?"—just share a personal story or use an "I" statement about why this project is important to you. This technique will serve as your silver bullet.

Tip #3: Start with the Big Picture

Whether you're competing against a worthy opponent at a management committee meeting or delivering a formal presentation, give an overview before launching into the details. Analyzers, including attorneys and other professionals who lead with the left side of the brain, are notorious for building a case or constructing an argument by delivering a pattern of facts. To be convincing, reverse the order and start with the gist or whole idea. This is the way our brains are hardwired and how we best process information.

> Start with the gist or whole idea. This is the way our brains are hardwired and how we best process information.

Another tendency of communicators, especially when they're feeling on the defensive or vulnerable, is to include too many facts or figures or give too much background information under the guise of establishing context. This is what we refer to as TBU: true but useless details. It's a tough habit to break.

We often prep executive management on presentations to prospective clients, boards, or shareholders. We regularly find them mired in trivia.

In one instance, three departments were engaged in a back-and-forth of emails regarding a press release to be delivered by the CEO. Right up until the day before the release of their quarterly earnings report, department heads were still submitting minor changes and corrections. There were endless debates over points of grammar, particularities of the message, and even choice of verbs, such as "poised" versus "ready." Is it any wonder that the CEO had trouble delivering his message, which was still in flux minutes before going before the public and press? Many pitches have washed up on these rocky shoals. Sometimes the outcome is critical.

> ***Fredericka*** *was hired to defend a suspect accused of murder. The accused had been a pillar in the community, serving as an officer on the local police force for many years. There was no murder weapon, no body, and no witnesses. And once his wife disappeared, he had been solely responsible for raising their children.*
>
> *On all counts, it should have been a straightforward case. But because it was Fredericka's first murder case, she made the mistake of copying how the prosecutor constructed opening and closing arguments. Instead of leading off with the big picture assumption of innocence and creating a positive impression of her client, Fredericka delivered a detailed time line that she believed would convince the jury that her client couldn't possibly have committed the crime.*
>
> *Her approach was ineffective. The jury found him guilty. Eight years later, he's still in prison and his children have neither a mother nor a father in their lives.*
>
> *When questioned afterward, jury members admitted that they were overwhelmed with the minutiae of dates, times, and places. Fredericka was doing her best to defend her client, but she got bogged down in details instead of telling a story that would portray her client as an innocent person wrongly accused of the crime.*

Try not to go too deeply into the weeds. Doing so takes your eye off the goal. Focus on your Intention and be single-minded about pursuing it. The details aren't nearly as important to your audience or opponent as they may seem to you. *Certainly* get the facts right, but deliver the big picture in a self-assured, focused, and comfortable manner. This is the key to being persuasive.

Tip #4: Be Brief, and Stick to the Point

Take a page from the litigator's playbook. Whether you're working with a small group or individually with a client, keep an eye on the flow of energy and make sure the dialogue is immediate and constant. It's particularly crucial to have an interactive conversation when you're pitching someone for new business. If you fail to notice when others want to enter the conversation, or make it about *you* rather than *them*, you risk not achieving your Intention. When a potential client hasn't participated in the meeting and concludes it with a cool "thank you," don't expect business referrals or an ongoing relationship.

If you fail to notice when others want to enter the conversation, or make it about *you* rather than *them*, you risk not achieving your Intention.

A prosecutor will often act concerned and keep asking a witness questions until the witness reveals something that's unintentionally or potentially damaging. It's the same in an IRS audit. Every good accountant will tell her client to answer only the auditor's specific questions and to say as little as possible. It's never a good idea to include supporting information, even if you *think* you're helping your case.

In business negotiations, the same rule applies. Don't give your opposition any ammunition that can be used against you. Remember that there's only so much information anyone can process at one time. If you speak too long or include too many concepts or details, the listener might not recall what you're saying, or miss your most important point.

Keep your answers brief and targeted. Speak in short sentences, so the listener can process what you've said. And pay heed to author George Orwell, who said, "Never use a long word where a short one will do."[94]

I remember producing videos to train emergency medical dispatchers. When a crisis happens—a child falls into a swimming pool or someone is having a heart attack—dispatchers are trained to ask the caller specific, vital questions to assess the proper course of action. In such an emotionally charged situation, callers can scream, babble, or insist an ambulance be sent immediately—if the dispatcher doesn't practice repetitive persistence. A skilled dispatcher will calmly repeat the question ("How old is the child?" "How long has your husband been unconscious?") until the caller is able to answer it.

Try the same tactic in a heated discussion (yes, you can do this without being annoying). If the person you're talking to isn't answering your question, and you believe that having an answer is essential before you take a course of action, repeat your question calmly and persistently until he responds.

Litigators also use repetitive persistence: They'll ask the same question multiple times until the witness becomes so upset or frustrated that he reveals something he shouldn't have—or at least that's what always happens on television.

Have you ever found yourself next to someone who just can't shut up? When you signal your discomfort, that person will often talk more—and faster. This condition is borderline logorrhea and can show up in meetings, presentations, and even informal conversation. It's usually triggered by nerves, and might stem from insecurity over not being engaging or persuasive enough. When someone feels she's expected to be witty, entertaining, or likable, words can cascade like a rushing waterfall.

Individuals who don't trust silence will fill the space like a disc jockey avoiding dead air.

Instead, honor the pause. A few seconds of silence not only gives you time to gather your thoughts and prepare what to say next, but also serves important functions for the listener. A pause allows someone to process what you just said. During a debate, a pause can make your opponent nervous. In business negotiations, traditional wisdom is that "She who speaks first, loses."

Do your best to monitor how long you've been speaking. If necessary, apply the brakes. Breathe, pause, and remind yourself to keep your remarks brief. There's almost always time for follow-up. And remember what you want to achieve. Keep your Intention top of mind.

Tip #5: Be Convincing

I frequently observe presenters hell-bent on educating their audience, even though the venue demands persuasion. When educating is your primary focus, two things are likely to happen—you put undue pressure on yourself to become the expert. And there is a greater tendency to speak too long, ramble, or throw the kitchen sink at your audience to prove your competence. Case in point:

Madeline has always been close to her mother, Joyce. Even though Joyce lives an hour away, Madeline takes her mom to lunch or a movie a couple of times a month, and they talk on the phone every morning. But when Joyce's memory started to deteriorate, and she could no longer drive safely or remember to turn off the stove, Madeline knew it was time to have that dreaded conversation.

Madeline jumped into "problem-solving mode." She researched assisted-care facilities in her neighborhood, visited the top three, and created a spreadsheet of what each had to offer. She then presented her findings to Joyce, carefully referencing attractive amenities such as apartment size, daily activities, and on-site medical care. She even broke out the costs of each facility, including meals.

The longer Madeline talked, the more upset Joyce became. She was livid that her own daughter would want to "put her away" because she was suddenly incapable of handling her own life. They argued for the entire lunch with no resolution at the end of the hour—or for that matter, over the next few weeks. Whenever Madeline brought it up, Joyce changed the subject. Finally, they stopped speaking to each other.

Distraught, Madeline asked me what to do. I recommended she drop the subject of moving her mom. Instead, I encouraged her to tell Joyce how much she meant to her. I said she could tell her mom how concerned she was that if she continued to live alone, she might hurt herself, and Madeline would feel it was her fault.

I suggested she ask Joyce what she thought would be a good solution and talk about options such as getting help (if Joyce could afford it), bringing in meals on Sunday for the entire week, or at the very least, hiring a cleaning person.

If Joyce brought up the subject of moving to an assisted-care facility, Madeline could say, "From a selfish perspective, I want you to enjoy this stage of your life with activities and friends nearby. And we could spend more time together if you lived closer to me." I told Madeline to listen, and truly hear Joyce's fears.

When we educate rather than persuade, we leave the door open to debate and pushback. The listener, like Joyce, will argue over the veracity of the details and specifics. Instead, it's more effective to talk about shared values, what moves us, and how a decision *feels*. Madeline and Joyce found common ground over how much they cared for one another. The subject of moving into assisted care has been tabled for now, but Madeline brought in a cooking-and-cleaning service to take care of her mom when she couldn't be there.

Talk about shared values, what moves us, and how a decision *feels*.

In *Influence: The Psychology of Persuasion*, Robert Cialdini wrote about common automatic response patterns that are encoded in human behavior and how easily these responses can be triggered. He cited research by Harvard social psychologist Ellen Langer showing that people complied with a request if they heard words that sounded reasonable, especially if they were given a plausible reason for the request.[95] For example, simply asking someone if you could cut in line usually doesn't work. But if you give a reason ("My friend is holding a space for me" or "I really have to go to the bathroom"), you're more likely to hear "Yes." In fact, when people were presented with a request *and* a reason, 94 percent complied, compared to only 60 percent when given a request only.[96]

For speakers and communicators, support your call to action with credible evidence. Tell your listeners *why* you want them to take action. Too often we feel that our rationale is obvious, but unless you supply a reason backed by well-chosen specifics, you won't trigger the automatic response patterns that govern behavior. Why settle for a 60 percent success rate, when you can move into the 94 percent zone?

Support your call to action with credible evidence. Tell your listeners *why* you want them to take action.

Tip #6: Don't Take It Personally

Crying, whining, or complaining makes women appear weak and unprofessional. Shed your tears in private. Put on your game face in public, especially when a lot is riding on the outcome.

> **Emma** *came to me because she was feeling ineffective at dealing with school officials responsible for her daughter, Olivia. The meetings were supposed to be a time for Olivia's team to discuss her needs, progress, and future goals as part of developing her Individualized Education Program (IEP). Even though Emma was a part of this team, she didn't feel that her contributions were valued, or even respected. She'd voice her opinion, but was often interrupted, put down, or ignored.*
>
> *A successful trial lawyer before having Olivia, Emma felt that being a stay-at-home mom for the past decade had eroded her confidence and heightened her anxiety.*
>
> *What made matters worse was that Emma was notified only a few days before these meetings. She was able to get a draft of the IEP document—but only the night before the meeting. That gave her little time to read over the proposed*

goals and think about how best to advocate for her daughter at the meeting the next day.

Emma felt intimidated at the meetings when officials used technical language or displayed a condescending attitude. No wonder her face turned red, her chest tightened, and her voice rose an octave whenever she attempted to speak.

During the most recent meeting, things were so contentious that Emma's thoughts became jumbled and she sounded angry.

Yet no matter how much she dreaded these meetings, Emma showed up every time. Without a unified game plan, Olivia would fail to receive the services she needed to grow and thrive. And that was unacceptable to this fighting mom.

First, I counseled Emma to be strategic and pick her battles carefully. For example, was the wording of a specific goal more important than the frequency of Olivia's occupational, physical, or speech-therapy sessions? Because Emma experienced frustration and agitation when remarks were directed to her, she specifically needed to focus on her Intention, or what she wanted to achieve. That way, she wouldn't take people's remarks personally. Keeping her Intention front and center meant Emma would be strategic, instead of reactive.

Since the annual IEP meetings were stressful, I recommended that Emma meet individually with team members before the next official meeting. She could then make an effort to form strategic alliances in a more relaxed setting, and find out more about what team members were thinking before she faced the large group.

I suggested Emma do the unexpected in the individual meetings and acknowledge the teacher or therapist for her positive work on Olivia's behalf. People enjoy getting credit, and once recognized, will be more open to giving you what you want next time. Just as important, Emma's voice would be less likely to betray her in these sessions, and she could speak more confidently about her daughter's needs. There's a huge difference between communicating one-on-one and facing a panel of decision makers.

Emma could also rehearse or role play before the big meeting by having a friend ask her tough questions, and then challenge her. This way, she could anticipate resistance and be prepared to address it calmly. Her goal should be to maintain control over her emotions.

Whenever possible, Emma needed to pause briefly, breathe, and then respond. If she needed to interrupt to insert her opinion, she should do so with diplomacy and firmness.

Because there was a ticking clock at the official meetings, I suggested Emma notify the organizer in advance that she'd like to share some concerns with the *team at the beginning. But she should make her remarks brief—this would require practice but would serve her in achieving her Intention.*

While speaking, Emma needed to make eye contact with the team members sitting at the table, be direct, and exude confidence—no matter how she was feeling inside. Staying calm and positive would impress the school team, and be an effective way of getting the group to pay attention to what she said.

Don't ever allow others to control the rhythm of your responses. And know that when you allow anger into the picture, you lose. There is no difference between pitching a major investment deal and making a better life for your child or parents. You control your fate.

Don't ever allow others to control the rhythm of your responses.

When David trained red-tailed hawks for falconry, it was a long, trying process. Pieces of raw chicken were fed to the fledgling with an accompanying whistle, as the bird was encouraged to advance down a perch and follow David's commands. The introduction of each new task was greeted with head-bobbing, swaying, and a rising shriek. These were physical signals of the bird feeling tense when made to do something new.

Eventually, the bird calmed down, learned the skill, and was rewarded. Humans behave much the same way when learning new communication skills; they exhibit anxiety "tells." These include the pitch of your voice (it will rise), movement such as rocking back and forth, and crossing your legs or arms in a protective stance. But we can see what the hawk can't: the reward of generating business through our ability to speak more effectively, and the confidence that our intentions will be realized. I'm not comparing birds to humans, but there's a valuable lesson here.

Tip #7: Leave the Past in the Past

If your goal is to win, consider what you can do from this point forward. Building a case based on how someone was wrong or treated you poorly won't change the outcome. Also, if you *expect* an interaction to be contentious, you'll be stressed, defensive, and will experience confirmation bias: "I knew he'd criticize my report, and sure enough, he did." Consider Emma, from the previous example, who needs to put the past behind her when she attends her next school meeting and advocates for her daughter.

Fortunately Emma isn't a celebrity, so she doesn't have the added burden of the world viewing her every move. In the 2012 Olympics, the swimmer Michael Phelps entered undiscovered territory. He was crushed by rival teammate Ryan Lochte, barely qualified in the 400-meter individual medley, and came in fourth in the final race. It was the first time Phelps had failed to medal in an Olympic event since 2000. His comments to the NBC commentator were clumsy at best. After a long pause, he sputtered, "It was just a crappy race" and "It's frustrating, it's upsetting . . ."[97] Then he abruptly exited. When you're twenty-seven years old, in the global spotlight, with your life and next career ahead of you, a bad stumble can damage your brand—even if you follow it with wins and more medals, which Phelps did.

Anyone who has achieved success has also experienced failure. How we behave and speak at moments of defeat is critical. Olympic medals are forever, but service contracts expire, providers fall out of favor with clients, and new opportunities may disappear. Effective communication reflects grace under pressure. If we conduct ourselves admirably in good times and bad, we'll always be perceived as winners.

If we conduct ourselves admirably in good times and bad, we'll always be perceived as winners.

Tip #8: Know They Might Be Wrong

Unfortunately, there are far too many critics and bullies in the press, management, and even our own families. I've had a number of clients come to us because they can't afford to leave their jobs but are miserable after being harassed, criticized, or treated unfairly. There are things you can do to ameliorate the situation, especially if changing your job or position isn't an option.

Talia is an experienced certified public accountant who now works as a book-keeper. Living in a small town, she has limited possibilities and sometimes has to put up with clients who give her a hard time or don't pay their bills.

She told me about her struggles with Alex, who owns a small sign company. His firm has had ups and downs, and Alex would take out his frustrations on Talia. She so disliked his verbal bullying that she quit working as his bookkeeper. When Alex begged her to come back, Talia agreed on one condition—that she could work remotely. This was a brilliant solution.

Talia took control by defining the conditions she would and would not accept. She wouldn't be subject to his verbal taunts in person at the office, where she felt like she couldn't escape from him. And, because Alex now knows that Talia is willing to walk away, he has cut back on his rambling, repetitive phone conversations. And when he does phone, Talia has the option of letting his calls go to voice mail and returning the call when it's convenient for her.

If you and your client disagree, you don't need to be arrogant and sound like the world's greatest authority. Simply saying "In my opinion" or "I have a different perspective" or "This is how I look at it" is respectful and will serve you well.

And whenever you know a client or opponent has a valid objection, do your best to get there first and address it. Don't try to gloss over or shove the elephant under the rug. In the movie *8 Mile* the rapper B-Rabbit, played by Eminem, beat out rapper Papa Doc. Rabbit knew Papa Doc would poke fun and put him down by talking about his character living in a trailer with his mother, getting his girlfriend pregnant, and basically being a loser from the wrong side of the tracks. But by getting there first, Rabbit left Doc with nothing to say. End of story.

Tip #9: Ask Questions and Dig for Specifics

How do you make sure every participant is engaged in a conversation or pitch? I frequently have clients tell me they're not good at networking or small talk and dislike sales—a lot. You don't need to be born a great salesperson to generate business or form strategic alliances. There's no magic to it. Whenever and wherever you meet people, ask what they're curious about.

Most people love to talk about themselves, and believe you're the best thing since sliced bread when you ask *them* a question, listen to their answer, and then say your version of, "Tell me more."

At our Eloqui trainings, we do an exercise called Active Cueing and Listening. The goal is to quickly build rapport and trust by putting your full attention on someone else. The instructions for this exercise are simple. Partner up with someone you don't know well. Each of you has five minutes to answer the following question: "What was a disappointment or setback in your life that had a positive outcome?" Other possibilities include, "Who was your coach or mentor, and what did you learn from that person that you've applied to your life?" Or, "Tell me about a success you're proud of." These questions are geared toward accessing both the right and left brain, because they require emotional and analytical responses.

The goal of Active Cueing and Listening is to quickly build rapport and trust by putting your full attention on someone else.

In the first five minutes, as the interviewer, it's your job to ask specific questions that delve deeper into the thinking and perspective of your partner. Don't allow a simple "yes" or "no" answer. Draw out details so you can picture the person's response. Repeat back every so often what you're hearing: "If I understand you correctly, you mean . . ." or "Is what you're saying . . . ?"

To go even deeper, you can say, "I've never experienced that; how did you deal with it?" or "I can't imagine what that's like. What happened?" Don't sound judgmental by saying, "You didn't really do *that*, did you?"

Borrow from improvisational artists, who can take a random statement or prop and build something wonderful on it. If you've ever watched the television show *Whose Line Is It Anyway?*, you'll be amazed at how quickly the performers create funny, intricate scenes. One technique they use is "Yes, and . . ." instead of "No, but . . ." By thinking "Yes, and . . ." the performer builds on the original idea her partner started. But when one of them says the equivalent of "No, but . . ." the scene stalls.

After four minutes, summarize what your partner told you in the last remaining minute. Then switch and let your partner interview you.

Take the lessons learned from this exercise into every communication. The fuel for keeping any conversation moving forward is specifics. Generalities such as "focused solutions" or "full-service firm" might make sense to you, but your audience can't picture these terms. Instead, be straightforward and employ concrete, descriptive, and specific language.

Whether you're at a networking meeting, your son's school, or an industry conference, stay present. Resist the temptation to turn the conversation back to you by saying, "That's interesting, because the same thing happened to me!" as a way to talk about yourself. Of course, in real conversation you eventually want to describe what you do or what's important to you. And your time will come—as humans, we're hardwired for reciprocity, so there'll eventually be a moment when the other person will say, "Tell me about you." Since you've been listening closely to the other person and asking probing questions, you'll know exactly which story or service to talk about. There's no better way to promote your services. If you're a manager supervising an employee, asking her for specific details of the situation or challenge will build your understanding and prompt her to solve the problem herself.

Sydney worked at a major toy company and was so dynamic in our group training that we knew she was destined for a leadership role. Sure enough, six months after we finished the training, we learned she had been promoted to a management position.

Sydney brought us in for coaching because she was having trouble managing the same people who'd been her equals just a few months before. It wasn't that they didn't respect her. It was that Sydney thought her job was to solve their problems whenever they came into her office.

Instead, when a staff member came in with a challenge, we advised Sydney to dig for specifics. Interestingly enough, the more the staff member described the problem, the more likely the person was to come up with a solution on her own.

Tip #10: Listen More Than You Speak

I saved the best for last. In tip number nine, I explained the Active Cueing and Listening exercise. After digging for specifics, repeat back what the other person has said in your own words. How else will your partner know that you've understood her correctly?

After digging for specifics, repeat back what the other person has said in your own words.

When conducting this exercise, I'll often hear someone repeat back what she thought she had heard, and her partner will say, "That's about right, but in addition . . ." It's not about being correct or perfect. Through clarification, the two individuals have elevated their understanding of each other to another level and become closer. A masterful interviewer can earn valuable trust in minutes.

Working across many industries, the number-one client complaint we hear is not feeling heard. Many deals are lost because the salesperson or vendor sold her services, instead of listening carefully, asking questions, and addressing the client's true concerns. When we wrote *Own the Room* and were interviewing public relations firms, I was shocked at how many made assumptions about what we wanted the book to do. They never asked questions or repeated back what we said in their own words. They assumed we were like other authors so they went on autopilot when discussing their services.

Instead of doing what the publicists did to us, paraphrase what the client has described as her challenge. Then go deeper with follow-up questions to elicit specifics. Only when you've truly grasped the meaning of the client's words can you propose a customized solution. By folding in what you've heard, you can effectively meet the client's needs.

Teddy, a financial advisor, is an Accelerator who loves doing sales and converting leads or prospects into clients. She went into a meeting with Joe, a soon-to-be-retired police officer. Within seconds, she believed she understood his financial needs for retirement and thought the meeting went well. Afterward, she sent Joe a proposal describing how she'd invest his money.

But Joe didn't return her calls. Eventually, he agreed to another meeting. Teddy didn't close him at that meeting, either. Ready to give up, I recommended that Teddy call Joe and apologize. Specifically, I suggested she tell Joe that because of her excitement over what she could accomplish for him, she hadn't really listened to him. This admission earned Teddy another meeting.

My recommendation was that Teddy spend time asking Joe questions and letting him answer—at length. She called me afterward, dumbfounded. "I signed him, but I never TALKED. How does he know what I'll do?" That's the wrong question. She'd persuaded Joe to become a client because he was finally assured that she'd listen and do what's best for him.

Rather than striving to be the expert and doing most of the talking, Teddy did the right thing at the third meeting. She drew Joe out and discovered what made *him* tick. Active Cueing and Listening is also an effective icebreaker, and will give you the best shot at turning any monologue into a dialogue. It's a great tool for any networking event or meeting.

Show your respect for others in all of your interactions. Drop any sign of attitude that might bleed into your tone, especially if you're frustrated or need to repeat yourself. Be a good listener, even when someone disagrees with you or is quiet and unresponsive. No matter how certain you feel about an issue, even those who disagree are entitled to their opinion.

In *Blink*, Malcolm Gladwell cited a study that identified driving factors in medical malpractice suits. The study found that when a physician spent an extra *three* minutes with patients and focused on active listening, the physician would be perceived favorably and was less likely to be sued. The same was true if the physician had a warm tone instead of a dominant one. The most successful technique was for physicians to orient the patients by describing or walking them through an upcoming procedure or treatment. When they did that, those physicians were almost immune to malpractice suits.[98]

Consider this phenomenon when speaking to clients. Like Teddy, we tend to rush to deliver a solution and focus on sounding assured, confident, and ready to proceed. But we may be hurting our chances to seal the deal, much less form a lasting, strategic alliance. When we fail to listen, be thoughtful, or ask pointed questions, the client doesn't feel heard. Favoring a commanding over a collegial tone adds salt to the wound. Unless we use concrete language, explaining the nuts and bolts of how we operate, we're vulnerable to competitors. As the malpractice study showed, we do ongoing business with those we know, like, and trust. Spend the time to earn that trust.

We do ongoing business with those we know, like, and trust. Spend the time to earn that trust.

I'm often asked the question, "Can someone really change and be success-ful at bringing in business?" Absolutely. The expectation of what a rainmaker should be is often the problem. In my experience, the skills that drive business do not depend on the gift of gab or finely tuned salesmanship. The secret is to ask incisive questions, listen, and give thoughtful responses. Rather than striving to be a silver-tongued devil, make insightful interviewing (or Active Cueing and Listening) your goal.

Trust is established through the mix of empathy and understanding. And when you engage in this focused dialogue, clients will be more receptive to hearing your story, because they won't feel sold to. You can be a magnet by your interest in and concern for others.

11

PERCEPTION IS REALITY: REPROGRAMMING OUR MIND-SET

Be open to absorbing new techniques and ways of operating. Set aside fear, be introspective about your unique qualities, and trust that you have the power to persuade.

You'll notice a theme throughout this book: the best speakers persuade rather than educate. Consider which approach is more likely to be successful in the following scenarios:

- You're a life insurance agent who thinks her company should expand its services to include financial consulting. Do you pitch the other agents in the firm to gain consensus, or would informing them produce the same result?

- At a monthly sales meeting, did you report last year's numbers, or did you interpret the numbers to motivate your team to increase sales in the next quarter?

- As the CEO delivering a PowerPoint presentation to your board of directors, did you update them on what has transpired since the last meeting? Or did you provide strategy about the prospects going forward, support your argument with colorful examples, and persuade them to approve your budget?

Even in our personal lives, it's easier to achieve our objective when we use persuasion. Did your partner agree to embark upon a costly makeover of your kitchen simply because you wanted a new project? Or were you able to convince him by explaining how it would increase your home's resale value and how wonderful you'd feel with added space to prep for dinner parties?

The difficulty for speakers stems from the belief that it is their responsibility to educate, inform, and then make sure the audience understands the topic. With this perspective, there is always the potential to add more content, especially if you want to be as thorough as possible. And your anxiety ramps up when you consider the possible negative responses from the listener who may know more than you do, or react negatively.

Say you're in an audience and the speaker pulls up her first PowerPoint slide. The image is dense with charts and figures. What goes through your mind? When I see or hear dozens of facts and start to feel overwhelmed by data, I don't care who the speaker is. I'm irritated by the prospect of having to sit through another dull presentation that promises nothing new or insightful. Even if the speaker is experienced and competent and I'm interested in the material—or required to attend for continuing-education credits—no one likes to be inundated by statistics. We don't learn when we're bored.

When informing is the sole purpose of your presentation, you put enormous pressure on yourself to become an Expert qualified to speak on the subject. Your material will likely be sanitized, lacking visual imagery and personal perspective that can sway the audience. The presentation will probably go on too long to sustain audience interest. Finally, you'll sound professorial, rather than like someone who is engaging and animated. As a result, it will be difficult if not impossible for you to achieve your Intention.

***

> When informing is the sole purpose of your presentation, you put enormous pressure on yourself to become an Expert.

Time and time again clients protest that they aren't comfortable adding their own perspective and insist on writing out the content and then reading it word-for-word during the presentation. They truly believe that their job is to educate rather than persuade their audience, client, or customer. I hear the same justification regardless of the person's industry, level of experience, or communication style.

*Recently I was on a call with **Jill**, an executive at a national insurance company. She needed to explain how a new computer system would shortcut invoicing and billing for field producers processing claims—but didn't want to sound "boring and technical."*

To make matters worse, she had to deliver this presentation as a webinar. People would be watching her on a screen—when they weren't distracted by others or checking their email while "listening."

When I asked her how she was going to open, Jill said she wanted to jump right into educating the producers on the features and functionality of the new system. Her true Intention was to convince the audience that this system was easy to use and would streamline the billing process, saving valuable time.

I persuaded Jill to start with the big picture. Together we crafted an opening example of how a producer stuck in a snowstorm couldn't make it back to the office in time to send out his monthly billing statements. Thankfully, since he'd switched to the new system and had pre-programmed the invoices, he was covered—the statements would be sent out automatically. This story was clear and concise. The audience could easily relate to the dilemma and solution.

We also discussed ways to describe the old and new systems. Jill could say that the old method of billing was like the Pony Express and the new system like Federal Express, when it "absolutely, positively has to get there overnight." Or the old system was like an ancient manual Olivetti typewriter that required correction tape to fix a mistake, while the new system was innovative like a touch screen.

By the time we finished, I could hear the excitement in Jill's voice as she realized she could convince her producers of the benefits of the new system, rather than merely educate them on its various functions.

Typically, success is achieved when the listener buys in, changes her perspectives, and takes action. While it's necessary to share your knowledge, it's best to think of each nugget of information as an ingredient used to assemble a fine paella. Eaten separately, the fish, sausage, rice, and seasonings each have a distinctive taste and texture. But artfully combined, the ingredients produce something wonderful. And in the best dishes, no one ingredient stands out—the flavors balance each other perfectly. The same is true for outstanding presentations. One way to achieve this perfect balance is by using similes, metaphors, or analogies the way that Elaine did.

> **Elaine,** an executive with a leading toy company based in Canada, was tasked with persuading General Motors to assign a new vehicle to the toy company's popular line of model cars. Understanding how long this process typically takes, Elaine decided that a win for her would be getting a second meeting with the GM executives.
>
> In preparation, Elaine listed all the selling points and benefits to GM if it assigned another vehicle. Then she documented the successful sales figures for previous GM cars in the product line. Her logic was impeccable. She was thorough and informed.
>
> I reviewed Elaine's PowerPoint as she rehearsed her speech. Although I usually DO NOT recommend using PowerPoint for the opening, this was different—I was intrigued by her concept and creativity.
>
> In the first image, Elaine filled the screen with a giant photo of a young boy driving a soapbox car. He was clearly having the time of his life. Her comments accompanying the slide were simple and direct: "Boys who love cars . . ."
>
> The second image was of talk-show host Jay Leno in the cockpit of a Formula One race car. This time Elaine's comment was, ". . . grow up to be men who love cars." She couldn't wait to deliver her pitch to GM.
>
> Sure enough, when the day came and Elaine projected her opening slides, the execs smiled. The key decision maker held up his hand, stopping Elaine from continuing. "How many cars would you like?" he asked.

In less than thirty seconds, Elaine had achieved her ultimate objective of persuading the executives to assign new car models—which was much more than getting a second meeting. The rest of Elaine's comments were set dressing. Her persuasive approach struck a chord. Her tactic was more successful than simply presenting data.

Remember Eloqui's motto: "If you educate people, you get them to think. If you persuade them, you get them to act." When you persuade an audience, your enthusiasm is effortless and your commitment is apparent.

"If you educate people, you get them to think. If you persuade them, you get them to act."
—Eloqui motto

BANISH THE IMPOSTOR

There's a scoundrel that's taken up residence in far too many female clients and colleagues. This inner critic tells them that they're not good enough, that what they have to say isn't important, and that someone else, hell, *anyone* else would be better at speaking in public than they are. This nasty creature always sounds so damn certain. Worst of all, it feels like a tug-of-war for women to counter these negative comments with logical, rational responses. Some might refer to this ominous being as the Ego. I call it the Impostor.

Jocelyn *had taken on the Herculean task of organizing the centennial celebration of her southwestern state. The project was short of funds and volunteers. The staff couldn't agree on who should be featured, which nonprofit should receive the proceeds raised through ticket sales, or how much tickets should cost.*

She handled these challenges like a seasoned politician, using her natural charm and extensive connections within the community. As the date of the event approached, Jocelyn obsessed over her remarks to welcome the attendees and acknowledge her committee. Her speech was only ten minutes, but in her mind they were the most critical moments of her life. She was convinced that she needed to memorize every word and deliver her remarks without notes or a teleprompter.

For that reason, Jocelyn and I decided a group presentation would be best. She went onstage flanked by her two committee members and let them do most of the talking. I sat in the audience and tried to give them telepathic support.

After all of our rehearsals and preparations, the most disappointing outcome had nothing to do with Jocelyn or her team's remarks. The audience was so noisy and impolite that they failed to give any of the three presenters the attention they deserved. After more than a year of volunteer efforts to pull off an incredible success, the three never had even a brief moment in the spotlight or received the accolades they richly deserved. To this day, Jocelyn avoids public speaking. It breaks my heart.

It's time to take a real look at the Impostor and tell it to take a hike. The Impostor thinks it's keeping us safe from danger or making a mistake. Instead, it's scaring us or making us brutally second-guess ourselves. The Impostor doesn't serve any useful purpose. We're bigger, smarter, and more than capable of exiling anything that wants to suck the lifeblood out of us. But it takes a determined effort to permanently silence this voice. I know I've said it before, but it's worth repeating. Every time the Impostor's critical voice pipes up, remind yourself of a past speaking success. It can be as insignificant as when you persuaded your teenage son to clean up his room or as notable as when you received positive evaluations and comments after a presentation at an industry conference.

> Every time the Impostor's critical voice pipes up, remind yourself of a past speaking success.

If the Impostor's voice is insistent, call in the troops. Go to one of your supporters and tell her what's happening. Many of the calls or emails I receive are from clients who start doubting their creative opening or their decision to tell a story with personal elements. Sometimes they're experiencing anxiety before a presentation and can't quiet the Impostor's voice. I remind them of how brave, articulate, and persuasive they are. I tell them how much better they are than they think they are. And I encourage them to take risks. They already know how it will turn out if they do it the same way they've always done it. But when you break new ground, there's a much a greater likelihood of success.

Valerie owned an insurance company and now heads a property-and-casualty division at another firm. For years, she'd avoided joining networking groups to advance her business because she was afraid her potty mouth (her term) would turn off potential clients. When I finally persuaded Valerie to join one anyway, some folks were turned off. But many others enjoyed her authenticity and became clients.

Recently, Valerie was asked to address a national conference on the mainstream application of drone technology and what needs to be included in insurance policies covering their use. Speaking in front of her peers was terrifying to Valerie, but she realized that her experience and knowledge of clients who'd used drones would be valuable to others. She appreciated how leading the way would set her apart and differentiate her services. So she faced her fears and accepted the speaking opportunity.

After we worked together, Valerie decided to frame her content by comparing The Jetsons, *her favorite childhood cartoon show, to the future of drone technology. This approach took what could have been a boring topic and made it fun for her and the audience. She received terrific reviews and has booked many more speaking engagements. Valerie is becoming the go-to person in her industry and her presentations put her in front of hundreds of potential clients at a time.*

Let's support any speaker who's brave enough to stand in front of an audience and speak; brave enough to share her thoughts, feelings, and opinions; and brave enough to take risks and break the old model of public speaking. When we band together, there's strength in numbers. The Impostor will have no place to hide. Good riddance.

TRUST YOUR INTUITION

To be a successful speaker or communicator, the most important thing you can do is put your full attention on the audience and what would serve them best. If you want to deliver value or drive others to take an action, trust your intuition and make your presentations creative, colorful, and specific. You may also need (heaven forbid) to change your material on the fly. And you'll need to employ a variety of techniques to keep an audience engaged. It all centers on what you want to achieve.

When I tell women to make an adjustment if they see that they're losing their audience, I often see a look of terror in their eyes: "Deviate from my script? Be spontaneous? Are you kidding? I'm not good at thinking on my feet." My response is: "You used to not be good at it." But that doesn't stop rebuttals like, "I need to know my content better before speaking about it," or my favorite, "Give me more time to be prepared, and I'll be better."

The truth is that the more time most speakers have to prepare, the more their presentations tend to be dull, lifeless, and ineffective. This is why Eloqui trainings include improvisational exercises that give participants only minutes to prepare. It's possible to build new skills and incorporate them into muscle memory without weeks or months of effort. Doing an improvisational exercise is a terrific way to come up with content that sounds natural and unaffected. I've been blown away by what women can create when they have only one minute to identify their Intention, take on a Role, or prepare a self-introduction based on a current event that they connect to their business.

One of the reasons we digitally record these exercises is so clients can review them later. Once the memory of the actual moment is past, participants can watch their DVD or digital file, reflect on what worked (or didn't), and appreciate the novelty of their responses. I want clients to recognize the benefit of spontaneity and connecting with an audience, rather than getting their information perfectly packaged and delivered. It's easy to have someone film you, with high-quality cameras embedded in smartphones.

There's another stumbling block to becoming a great communicator. If you rarely give presentations, you will tend to put too much pressure on yourself to make each talk exceptional. Give yourself the assignment to present whenever and wherever you can, including in low-risk environments such as meetings, moderating a panel, or social events. Then it won't matter if one particular presentation isn't your best. Speaking in public is like anything else you do regularly: The more you do it, the better you'll become.

> It's possible to build new skills and incorporate them into muscle memory without weeks or months of effort.

KNOW THYSELF

To become successful when you're out front, play to your strengths. Discover what makes you stand out from others in your field. What are your strengths and distinguishing characteristics? Zero in on what makes you unique. Consider where you've lived, your hobbies, other jobs you've had, sports you've played, what you learned from a mentor or coach. Once you've identified a potential differentiator, ask yourself how that quality benefits your client or audience. Since I was trained as a director, I can quickly identify my clients' strengths and weaknesses, and give them the tools to be successful in any "scene."

Whenever you have the chance, include your differentiators when speaking to your audience, customer, or client. I know. It sounds so easy to say. But when all eyes are on you, you feel like a bug trapped under glass. Tell yourself that the audience wants you to succeed.

Really take that in. Audiences want you to be engaging. And they want to hear something unique about you, your perspective, or your subject matter. The audience wants you to succeed. Listeners want to hear something unique that only you can deliver.

The audience wants you to succeed. Listeners want to hear something unique that only you can deliver.

We all possess the ability to become compelling speakers. We need technique, desire, and practice. Ask any seasoned professional. She'll tell you she wasn't born a great singer, dancer, comedienne, or actor. She learned her craft. She took risks and occasionally failed. She had a goal and kept her sights set on achieving it, regardless of the setbacks or obstacles along the way.

On a trip to Ojai, California, I visited **Juliette**, a ceramics artist, at her studio. I was admiring a beautiful pot she'd made. It had an intricate black-and-white design covering the entire surface, with carved lines and perfect symmetry. I asked her how long it took her to complete this exquisite piece. "Three hours and twenty-five years," she said. I knew exactly what she meant.

Juliette had put in years to learn her craft. When she produced a piece, it took her less time than when she was a beginner, and she didn't sacrifice quality. But she was also quite clear that it had taken years of practice and making mistakes to get to this point.

What makes you stand out? If answering this is difficult, take an aspirational approach. How you would like to be perceived? Mull that over and then put the building blocks in place to create that image. Ask those closest to you how they see you, and which of your qualities they respect and admire. Prime their responses by asking them the following questions:

- What sets me apart?

- What makes you pay attention to what I have to say?

- When do I sound the most animated, engaged, or connected to my topic?

- What distracts you from hearing or remembering my message?

- At what point do I lose you when I speak?

- What can I do to improve my presentations?

You can be an effective speaker whether you're reserved and thoughtful or animated and excited. You can have a quirky sense of humor with your own wacky take on a subject, and still be an effective speaker.

> *Adele took over as chairwoman of a legal association in southern California. A tireless advocate, she worked behind the scenes for those who couldn't afford legal services. Her new position also required her to be a leader and have a commanding presence. She knew that she'd need to speak at large events, including fundraisers and the annual benefit where fellow members, judges, and the press were invited.*
>
> *At her induction, Adele wanted to set herself apart from the retiring chair, who was more traditional in his appearance and speech. Adele's gravelly voice still retained a heavy Brooklyn accent and stood out in any crowd. This woman could project. If she chose to deliver her acknowledgments like her predecessor, it would just sound wrong.*
>
> *At one of our coaching sessions, I learned what shaped Adele's personality and drive. Her Italian parents were Wobblies (Industrial Workers of the World) who influenced her career path. Her father was a retired longshoreman who still met his co-workers in a coffee shop every morning. Her mother prepared dinners for the extended family on weekends, making baked ziti and other Italian dishes from scratch.*
>
> *I encouraged Adele to weave in family stories to connect her vision of the association with her family history. We rehearsed the speech a number of times to make sure she slowed down and spoke clearly, so no one would miss a word.*
>
> *Her speech was not only a success, but also one of the factors that propelled her later to become head of the state bar association. More than eight years later, clients tell me that Adele's induction speech was the most colorful and inspirational talk they'd ever heard.*

While there's no one-size-fits-all definition of a great presenter, use variety to keep the audience engaged. That's why playing to your strengths is so important. Striving to be like anyone else is a mistake. Imagine a daylong conference with multiple speakers who all sound alike. That's my definition of Hell.

12

MANAGE ANXIETY AND DELIVER LIKE A PRO

Reducing your anxiety and rehearsing your material mutually reinforce each other. Take a page from performers who constantly have new content to construct, learn, and deliver to audiences.

THE UPSIDE OF ANXIETY

It's not just you. Most people suffer from speaker anxiety. Since stage fright is such a pervasive condition, you may wonder why I've waited until near the end of the book to focus on it. In my years of coaching and training clients, I've found that speaker anxiety can be greatly diminished simply by speaking on a regular basis and having the right tools in place when anxiety rears its ugly head.

Here's what you may not realize. You don't want to eliminate stage fright altogether. Anxiety is a great editing device. The synapses in your brain are firing and everything is in sharper focus. You can think more quickly on your feet and read the room more effectively. Audiences can tell that you're engaged and ready to go. Many theatrical performers, at the top of their game, will hurl before going on stage—but that means their performance is important to them.

If you no longer feel an accelerated heartbeat or dry mouth or other symptoms of stage fright, that's when it's time to worry. We like to say, "Buddhist monks are boring." When a client tells me that she wants to be calm before speaking, I do my best to dissuade her.

You want some anxiety, but it needs to be managed. You never want to be overwhelmed, dominated by fear, or feeling as if you're having an out-of-body experience (just ask the actor Shirley MacLaine[99]). If you feel light-headed and can't put together a rational thought before you begin to speak, then your stage fright is too intense.

You don't want to eliminate stage fright altogether. Anxiety is a great editing device.

There are many causes of stage fright. The top three are when you're faced with a surprise or something unexpected happens, when you're unprepared or feeling that way, or when you believe there's a lot riding on the outcome of your presentation. For women, I'd add a fourth: when you fear that you'll be judged. Let's tackle these problems.

EXPECT THE UNEXPECTED

I can't stress enough how valuable it is to be prepared and organize your content. Create an outline with large fonts and lots of white space. Have a backup plan in case of equipment failure. And rehearse in the space (or an equivalent) where you will be presenting. You want to feel bulletproof, or the Seasoned Veteran equivalent of "Throw something at me. I can take it."

Surprises take many forms. Maybe you were told you'd have forty-five minutes, but shortly into your presentation the client tells you to "wrap it up in five." Or you expect to present to a handful of people, only to be ushered into a packed ballroom. Or perhaps you left your only copy of the outline on the plane, and didn't bring your laptop so you can't print it out again. You get the idea. Surprises happen to all of us. They're unavoidable.

For example, a new client had scheduled us as keynote speakers at an annual conference in Indianapolis. I got a phone call from our contact early Sunday morning wondering why we weren't registered at the hotel until Monday. I politely told her that we didn't need an extra day, since we were speaking on Tuesday. There was a long pause. Our contact person double-checked the schedule and said she didn't know how it happened, but we were definitely on the agenda to speak on Monday.

Being a Pragmatist, I said it was no problem (sounding more confident than I felt). I tracked down David and told him to get home as soon as possible. I located a flight that would get us into Indianapolis that night and tossed some clothes into a suitcase. We not only made it to the conference in time, but the president of the company also apologized profusely and thanked us for our flexibility. The result was that we earned brownie points and cemented a long-term relationship.

Surprises don't always work out that well. Years ago, one of the country's biggest software companies invited us to deliver a keynote at its conference. This is familiar territory for us, so we weren't concerned. However, the organizers kept asking for our PowerPoint, so it could be projected behind us. We told them that we don't use PowerPoint when we're training people to speak. Maybe it was because this company had developed the software program, but our response didn't go over well.

We went in for a scheduled sound check the morning of our keynote. David and I weren't happy with the audio in the empty room, but the engineer assured us that the sound would be different with a full house.

Unfortunately, the engineer was wrong. As we delivered our keynote later that day, the audio echoed and bounced off the walls. Our two microphones were turned up too high, causing annoying feedback. To make matters worse, when a participant stepped up to the floor microphone, we couldn't understand a word he said. We moved so close to the edge of the stage that we almost fell off. His muffled words sounded something like "chumniohwoiehhfhion."

Taking a stab in the dark, I gave him advice that would apply to most speakers. But his response was "I spent the last five minutes telling you *just* that." Attendees started leaving the auditorium.

Some days you can't win. Fortunately, now we laugh about it.

NOT ENOUGH TIME

What happens when you feel unprepared or you're asked to speak on a topic without adequate time to do research and craft a compelling presentation? As always, I recommend falling back on technique. Since Intention drives everything, spend a few minutes considering what you want to achieve. Then be creative about how best to accomplish it in whatever time is available to you.

When anxiety spikes and you're concerned about remembering your content or how you'll be perceived, remind yourself of your Intention. For example, in a pitch your Intention could be "We will partner together for a successful outcome." Or before a presentation your Intention could be, "They will see me as the go-to person in estate planning." Let your Intention become your mantra. Say it over and over again until it drowns out all other noise.

When anxiety spikes and you're concerned about remembering your content or how you'll be perceived, remind yourself of your Intention.

Another anxiety-reducing tool is to decide which Role you believe will allow you to achieve your Intention. In our Eloqui workshops, I'm frequently amazed at how Roles can transform even speakers who are shy or anxious. I'll ask a volunteer—with zero prep time—to stand up and speak on her topic through the filter of a Role such as Seasoned Veteran, Motivator, or Visionary. I instruct the volunteer not to be concerned with getting her facts right, because this is only an exercise.

Taking on a Role can give you magical powers. In addition to being more confident and expressive, the volunteer when put on the spot will invariably do a commendable job of organizing her material and persuading the audience. Without having any time to prepare, she's drawing upon her intuitive skills. But being female, the volunteer will often doubt herself, and might argue with me or deny that my feedback is accurate—until other participants in the room weigh in or I show her the exercise afterward on her DVD.

Other tools to reduce anxiety include choosing a personal opening that sets the frame, recalling an anecdote that brings your material to life, and selecting an appropriate and colorful close. Then always rehearse your open and close until they're solid.

TAP INTO A SENSE MEMORY

What can you do when there's a lot riding on the outcome? All the preparation in the world won't fix this problem. Anxiety can start days or weeks before the actual presentation and peak the day of or minutes before you deliver your remarks. In this case, the fear, discomfort, and worry can be extreme.

Please don't wait until anxiety is paralyzing or avoid speaking altogether. Start with sense memory, a technique used by athletes to enhance their performance as well as by actors trained by Sanford Meisner and the Neighborhood Playhouse in New York.[100] The concept is to recall an experience in which you exhibited the same quality you would like the audience to see—such as confidence, warmth, or enthusiasm. Once you've spent the time to create your sense memory, you'll be able to quickly recall it just before speaking.

Konstantin Stanislavsky of the famous Moscow Art Theatre believed his students needed to take emotion and personality to the stage and call upon it when playing their character. He also explored the use of objectives and empathizing with the character.[101]

These are the same qualities that compelling speakers exhibit when addressing an audience of one or a hundred.

Here's how sense memory works. Let's say you want to project confidence when you're pitching a new idea or speaking in front of an audience of your peers. Days before your presentation, put fifteen minutes aside, sit in a quiet space, and remember a time when you actually experienced that state of being—in this case, confidence.

> Sit in a quiet space, and remember a time when you experienced being confident.

Select one event or moment when you felt extremely confident. Maybe it was when you persuaded your neighbors to participate in a work program to beautify the garden in your development or after you completed your first marathon. Or perhaps it was when you closed a new piece of business that colleagues said was impossible to win.

Now close your eyes and take the time to fully recreate that moment. This is the long version. Go through all five senses and remind yourself of what that event looked, felt, tasted, smelled, and sounded like. Be as specific as possible until it is vivid and fresh in your memory. While you're creating your sense memory, grip your wrist with the other hand.

Then, ten minutes before your actual presentation, go to a quiet space, close your eyes, grab your wrist, and bring back your moment of confidence. This time, it should take you only seconds to recreate the sense memory, and you'll walk into your arena exhibiting a state of confidence.

Another technique from the performers' playbook is creative visualization. I'm not a big fan of picturing the audience naked. But I am a fan of picturing myself in front of a warm, receptive crowd. I imagine that I am compelling, clear, and engaging. Everyone is smiling and nodding in agreement. Sometimes, at the end of my speech, the crowd gives me a standing ovation. I tell myself that I will be gracious and appreciative of their positive response. And it feels wonderful.

Here are two other mind games that reflect my time in California and experience in the entertainment industry.

Be a tree (no, that isn't a typo). Sit in a quiet place, in a chair. Uncross your legs and plant your feet firmly on the ground. Close your eyes and place your hands on your thighs. Imagine your feet as roots of an oak tree, growing right through the floor and deep into the earth. Your body has weight and substance. This exercise counters the out-of-body feeling of light-headedness that comes with stage fright. And no one has to know what you're thinking.

The other exercise is called the Golden Orb. I use this exercise to exhibit excitement and energy when addressing an audience. About thirty minutes before a presentation, sit quietly and close your eyes. Now imagine a golden orb or light radiating out from the center of your being. This small, compact ball grows larger and larger until its light permeates your entire being and is transmitted out onto the audience. Feel the energy created by the orb. Use this energy to fuel your talk and focus your mind.

CHANGE YOUR INTERNAL MESSAGE

As women, we're often our own worst critics. We're harder on ourselves than anyone else. We dismiss positive comments as being false, on the basis that the person who gave us kudos did so as a friend.

This has to change. Successful speakers build positive memories to replace the negative ones. The next time you experience anxiety when you're asked to moderate a panel, deliver a toast at a wedding, or introduce a colleague at a conference, take the time to remember and applaud a former success. Go over this past speech, introduction, or event in your mind. Play it back the way you would a favorite scene in a movie.

When we recall negative memories, failures, or rejections, something physical happens to our bodies. We might slump in our chair, sigh, or feel beaten down. Scientists call this linking of like memories "mood congruity."[102]

But if we remember our success, we're encoding positive messages into our brains. We learn better and faster. We feel more confident about an upcoming presentation and have the expectation that we'll have another success or win. And best of all, we have less worry and anxiety.

> If we remember our success, we're encoding positive messages into our brains.

Of course, the opposite is also true. I've had clients tell me, "Last time I spoke, I didn't do so well. I'm worried it will happen again." In effect, they're right. If you dwell on failure, you will repeat failure. Better to focus on a success, no matter how small, and place it at the top of the queue in your memory to drown out the negative noise.

Another incorrect perception is that the audience is judging us harshly and wants or expects us to fail. Nothing could be further from the truth. With a few exceptions, audiences want a speaker to be good. They want to learn something new or hear a unique take on a topic. Most of all, audiences want to sit back and enjoy the ride, rather than share the speaker's anxiety.

When Sally Field accepted her Academy Award in 1985 for lead actress in *Norma Rae*, she said, "I haven't had an orthodox career, and I've wanted more than anything to have your respect. The first time I didn't feel it, but this time I feel it, and I can't deny the fact that you like me, right now, you like me."[103] Her sentiment sounded a bit needy, but she was correct.

Probably the biggest obstacle women need to overcome is our tendency to self-monitor. It's impossible to be focused and think on our feet while worrying about how we're doing or being perceived.

When we're addressing an audience or client, we have to turn off the critic in our heads. You know the voice. It chatters incessantly: "You just forgot a key selling point. You're losing the audience. You're weak on the valuation section. You're gonna blow it." There's no faster way to tank your performance than listening to this voice. When you're speaking, your ONLY job is to focus on your audience and achieve your Intention. Everything else is a distraction.

> ## When you're speaking, your ONLY job is to focus on your audience and achieve your Intention.

BRING IT HOME

Now it's time to rehearse. It always surprises me when clients tell me they wing it when they deliver their presentations. Just the other night, a high-level government official told us that he knows his content, so all he needs to do is speak to the audience.

You're probably thinking that you wouldn't dream of speaking in public without extensive preparation. But it may surprise you to hear that there are speakers who believe they'll be more engaging if they make it up as they go along.

Never wing it! To me, that's like going out in a kayak on Lake Tahoe without first checking the winds, boat traffic, and impending weather. That is exactly what I did a few years ago. After spending an agonizing three hours paddling into the eye of a storm, I finally made it back to shore. I can't remember ever being so exhausted. But I learned my lesson. Knowing how to speak (or paddle) isn't enough. There are other factors to consider. And women, especially, like and need to be prepared.

A-list performers rehearse their material. But be careful of overrehearsing, because then your content can sound canned or memorized. The trick is finding the right balance of being prepared but not robotic.

Consider how tough it is for theater actors. They can't deviate from their script, but night after night, their job is to keep the material sounding fresh and their character believable.

Let's employ techniques from the actor's playbook:

1. **Modify the Wording and Phrasing**

   Do this each time you rehearse your content. Change the order. Not only will this refresh your material, but you may also discover a new and better way of expressing your ideas.

   If you don't change your content and you rehearse it exactly the same way every time, that's a problem for two reasons. First, you never want the audience hearing a memorized cadence in your voice. Second, what happens if you're in front of an audience, and you freeze and forget the next word? It's very hard to recover. No one wants that level of stress.

   Fortunately, if you've rehearsed your content somewhat differently every time, you'll be able to access it and find a way to keep going under any circumstance.

2. **Listen to How You Sound**

   Always, always, always rehearse your presentation out loud. It's amazing how different it sounds when you speak the words aloud, as opposed to going over the content in your head. I like speaking to the mirror when I rehearse, but this technique is distracting to others. For me, I am my own best audience, so the mirror is a friendly face.

   > Always, always, always rehearse your presentation out loud.

3. **Start in the Middle**

   Another performer's technique is to alter the starting point when you rehearse. Do you practice from the beginning and get to the end, or do you tire out about midway through? If you're like most of our clients, you tend to rehearse your opening multiple times, but *underrehearse* the last half to third of your presentation. Many people often ignore the close altogether. Audiences remember most what they hear last. So make sure to rehearse your finish or close as well as your opening.

4. **Practice on a Stage, if Possible**

   There's a concept in psychology called "encoding specificity."[104] As a speaker, that means rehearsing your talk in an environment closely approximating where you'll be presenting. For example, if you're speaking to an audience in a ballroom, rehearse in a space that's also quite large so you can practice projecting your voice and moving your eye contact around the room.

If you're delivering a pitch at a conference table, rehearse in a similar space. Sit at a table and imagine yourself speaking to the audience or client. When possible, begin your presentation standing and then sit to be more collaborative. Also, rehearse how you will interact with your PowerPoint.

5. The Scout Motto: Be Prepared

Don't leave anything to chance. Surprises are responsible for throwing a speaker off, especially when a lot is riding on the outcome. To reduce anxiety and give yourself the best possible result—be prepared. Have backup plans if your PowerPoint fails. Be ready if your time is cut in half or delayed. And whenever possible, visit ahead of time the space where you will be presenting. Anticipate changes and you'll never be thrown off course.

6. On-Site Dry Run

When I arrive at the hotel, my first stop is to check out the space where I'll be speaking. I decide whether I need a microphone or can project without one. I see how the chairs are configured and where I can walk without interfering with anyone's sight line. I move in the space, either on the stage or floor, and deliver my opening and/or closing remarks. I also imagine the audience responding positively to my words. If I need to make physical changes to the room, seating, or audio, I get it done immediately.

If you can't visit the space where you'll be presenting, ask your contact person how the room is configured. What are the anomalies? For example, are the walls thin so noise bleeds through? Is the room usually reserved for lectures and the rows are steep and high? Will a wireless lavaliere or handheld microphone be available? When it comes to audio, here's a tip for women: Wear a jacket, top, or dress made of material stiff enough to support the microphone so the fabric doesn't fold in against your skin or allow the mike to flop around. If you're wearing a dress, make sure you have a belt for the clip on the wireless battery pack.

7. **Test Your Equipment**

When you're using PowerPoint, be sure to test all of your equipment (including the remote) in the space where you'll be presenting. I guarantee that at some point it will fail or be incompatible with the existing system. Even if you use PowerPoint all the time, trust me on this one. The horror stories I've heard about PowerPoint or audio failures could fill another book. But don't worry. As long as you have a voice, you have backup. You can always count on you.

As long as you have a voice, you have backup. You can always count on you.

---

8. **Act It Out**

My heart goes out to the women who spend an inordinate amount of time researching, writing, and rehearsing their presentations. They've invested so much effort that speaking becomes a life-or-death endeavor. For them, there's nothing enjoyable about giving presentations.

If this sounds like you, there's something you can do to make the experience less intimidating or threatening. When rehearsing your talks, take on a character as different from yourself as possible. For example, if you're a quiet, shy introvert, pretend that you're an over-the-top, self-centered diva or a bad Las Vegas entertainer.

The point of this exercise is to mentally and physically free you. I've had clients tell me the fun they had rehearsing as outrageous characters bled over into the actual delivery of their presentation. They felt looser and more at ease, and enjoyed having permission to play and go outside their comfort zones. Just to be clear: these are *rehearsal* techniques. Once you're in front of your audience, deliver your material as you—not a fictional character.

9. **Spice It Up**

If you tend to repeat certain lines or phrases, such as your company mission statement or a description of your services, there are rehearsal techniques you can employ to freshen up this content.

First, say the words out loud and put the accent on all the wrong syll-AW-bles. Then, go back to saying your content in a normal voice, and observe how difficult it is to be rote in your delivery. That's a good thing.

Recite your text with a bad French or Italian accent. Sing the lines. Dance them. When theater actors have spent weeks memorizing and rehearsing their scripts, the director gives them these exercises, or has them paraphrase their lines to inject new energy and life into their line readings. As with any good performer, your goal is to keep your material fresh. The concept behind all of these rehearsal techniques is to trick your brain into hearing your material in a whimsical and unexpected way.

The concept behind all of these rehearsal techniques is to trick your brain into hearing your material in a whimsical and unexpected way.

Years ago, I was a keynote speaker at an annual forensic CPA conference. I was freaking out over it. I was going to do the usual team-presenting handoffs with David, but I didn't feel prepared, and the keynote was the next morning. Whenever I asked David to rehearse, he was obliging, but in the rehearsal, I could tell that he wasn't giving his best effort, and this frustrated me.

What David was doing is what performers call a "stumble through." Rather than giving his all in the rehearsal, he was marking the various sections and saving his best performance for the actual keynote.

Since that time, I've observed speakers who sound tired, bored, or not at their peak. I'll bet they gave away their best performance in a rehearsal and not when it counted. So in my stumble through, I'll say things like, "Here I give the gist of why storytelling is important, being part of our culture and creation myths, blah, blah, blah, and then I tell how stories are the silver bullet in marketing." One of the many reasons I've grown to love a stumble through is that it shows me which sections I know well and which need more work.

Professionals also use rehearsal time to determine what to emphasize and which comments to lift, or make more important, during the presentation. If you want your audience to remember key concepts or ideas, move beyond the trite line: "This is important." Instead, pause before and after a specific phrase. If you've been speaking softly, raise your voice (the opposite also works). Or repeat the line, exactly the same way or slightly differently. But don't say, "To repeat . . ." or "As I said . . ." Just do it.

What if you're afraid that, even with all this rehearsal, you'll forget what you wanted to say? It happens to everyone. And most of the time, what you forgot or left out wasn't that important anyway. The trick is not to beat yourself up over it or look so uncomfortable that the audience is uncomfortable for you.

Your greatest safety net is your outline. Take it on stage with you and place it nearby. Don't hold it in your hands or that's all the audience will see. Use a large font size for key words or phrases on your outline. That way, if you lose your place, you can glance down, catch a word or phrase, and then speak to the audience while maintaining eye contact. Make sure to finish a thought or sentence while looking out at the audience, and *then* glance down for what's next. Never look down and read your material line by line.

If you decide to present without notes and forget your place, employ the actor's secret weapon—the meaningful glance. If you lose your place, stop. Look down at the floor or an inanimate object (staring at a real person may throw you off). Take a few steps in any direction with a thoughtful, intense look on your face. This will buy you precious seconds to remember what you wanted to say next.

Another technique or safety net is to recap what you've said so far, even if you're only minutes into your presentation. Don't say, "To recap." Just give the highlights. By the time you get to the place where you blanked out, chances are you'll remember where you were and what you wanted to say next.

In a debate during the 2012 presidential race, Republican candidate Rick Perry forgot the third federal department he'd eliminate if elected.[105] He tried self-effacing humor and even asked his opponents—who, not surprisingly, weren't talking. Learn from his mistake. Rather than giving a specific number or list, keep it general and say, "There are departments I would eliminate that include . . ." That way, if you forget the third item on your list or, in Perry's case, the Department of Energy, no one is the wiser.[106]

Whoever does a lot of public speaking knows it's an odds game. At some point, you'll forget what you wanted to say or repeat yourself. When I'm feeling particularly gutsy and forget where I am, I'll say to the audience, "I want to be sure you are paying attention. Who can tell me where I was?"

If you want to own the room and speak out—take charge. Commit to giving a high-impact talk. Outline your presentation. Move in the space. Rehearse. And then do whatever is necessary to convince and engage the audience.

TAKE THE PLUNGE

You've accepted a speaking engagement, and today is the day. If your first thought when you wake up is, "Why didn't I rehearse more? I'm not ready"—stop it. Replace the negative message with a positive one and tell yourself some version of, "I'm excited. I'm ready. Send me in."

Go for a walk or a run, or do whatever exercise you enjoy if you have time. Stretch your arms and legs so you feel limber and loose. A physical workout will relax your muscles, make your breathing more regular, and give you energy. Oxygen will flow to your brain. While you're working out, you can rehearse your presentation one more time, go over your open and close, and do a final stumble through.

Leave yourself plenty of time to get to the location. Better to be early and get a cup of coffee than to be stuck in traffic and anxious that you will be late. While going to your location, warm up your voice. Move up and down the scales humming "Mmmm." Do voice and diction exercises such as saying, "Lily let Lucy" and "Lippity-Pippity" and over-enunciate the "t" sounds. Make your facial muscles more limber by saying, "OOO-Weet" and "Who-You." You want your instrument (i.e., voice) to be well tuned, so treat it well.

Stay hydrated by drinking room-temperature water. Apples and grapes also lubricate the voice. Avoid high-fat dairy, which can create excess mucous in your throat, as well as strong teas and carbonated drinks that can dry you out or create eruptions of gas.

Eat a normal breakfast, lunch, or dinner. However, if your presentation is scheduled during a meal or immediately afterward, I recommend that you eat lightly (eggs or yogurt for breakfast; protein and greens for lunch or dinner). You want to fuel your brain so your body can function properly and not spend crucial energy processing or digesting food.

SHIFT GEARS BEFORE YOU SPEAK

Thirty minutes before any presentation, bridge (or transition) from your normal activities to the speaking task at hand. If you don't have that luxury, take at least ten minutes. Clear your mind and get ready by doing the following steps:

- Pass off any obligations to a co-worker or write them down.

- Turn off your cell phone and laptop.

- Quiet your thinking.

- Practice breathing from your diaphragm. Breathe deeply and exhale slowly. This type of breathing will support your capacity for delivering longer sentences or sections of text.

- Mentally rehearse your opening with variation.

- Review the highlights of your presentation.

- Close your eyes, grab your wrist, and recall your sense memory.

Thirty minutes before any presentation, bridge (or transition) from your normal activities to the speaking task at hand.

If anxiety is still plaguing you, close your eyes and picture yourself in a favorite spot, such as a mountain peak or a gurgling stream. Imagine watching the sunset from your back porch. When you mentally place yourself in a calm environment, your body also calms down, especially when you remember to breathe.

SHOW TIME

You're in a state of readiness when your breathing is normal and adrenaline is coursing through your veins. You can think because you've oxygenated your brain. You've eliminated all distractions and turned on your microphone. Right before going on, focus on your Intention or repeat the mantra, "They need what I have to deliver."

Walk confidently onto the stage or into the conference room. Place your outline within reach. Look out and engage the listeners. This is your fan base. They're rooting for you.

Before launching into your presentation, pause and take a breath.

During your presentation, move your eye contact around the room and rest on one person for no more than a few seconds at a time. Change up where you direct your gaze, so that it isn't symmetrical. For example, look to the right, the middle, and then back to the right before moving to the left side of the room. Whenever possible, make sure to land important points by looking *at* an individual, rather than moving your gaze and diluting the impact of your statement.

Here's the tough part. You need to stay in the moment. Be self-aware, not self-critical. You don't have the luxury of critiquing or congratulating yourself as you present. The brain can only do one major task at a time. If you pay attention to the thoughts in your head, then your presentation will suffer.

> You don't have the luxury of critiquing or congratulating yourself as you present.

A speaker's job is to connect with the audience, which requires being in the moment, focused and outer-directed. If any mistakes occur, keep moving forward. You can debrief after the presentation.

RE-ENTRY: CONSTRUCTIVE FEEDBACK

You've finished, and your relief is palpable. Now you face the next hurdle. Don't let the *but* monster in. You know you did well, but after a few hours or the next day, doubts start to creep in ("I did all right, but . . ."). You remember something you wanted to say, *but* forgot. You expected to hear from your supervisor with congratulations, *but* she hasn't contacted you. Or the old perfection demon takes up residence in your head and you start doubting your performance.[107]

There are ways to silence this annoying creature and move forward. First, since you had an Intention, you know whether or not you achieved it. For example, if your Intention was to generate three new business contacts from your talk, how many people came up to you afterward, gave you their business cards, and asked for a meeting?

If your Intention was to be seen as the go-to person in your field, were you asked for your availability to speak to another audience?

Or if your Intention was to persuade a decision maker to buy in to your idea, did you achieve it?

Clients who are in sales will say to me that their Intention is always to close the business deal. But there are intermediary steps along the way. If your Intention was to qualify to see whether the fit is right to partner together, did that happen? Or, if you want a long-term relationship and your Intention was to get a second meeting, you know whether or not you achieved it.

Next, ask a colleague who attended your presentation the following questions.

1. What was my Intention?
2. What do you remember from my presentation? (Ask for specifics.)
3. How can I improve?

Then thank the colleague for giving his or her comments and insights. If you like, prep the person ahead of time with the questions you will be asking.

And if you know you could be better, but can't grasp the process, reach out to a professional. When interviewing a speaker coach, make sure he or she is field trained and has worked with professionals at your level. Make sure the coach customizes the program to you and isn't simply following a manual. And make sure your personalities resonate, because revealing your fears and accepting coaching comments can make anyone feel vulnerable. You need to trust the coach's opinion.

Finally, attaining mastery is a process. When you've decided to improve your game, don't place your expectations so high that they're impossible to achieve. In my fifteen years of coaching and training hundreds of individuals, I have yet to meet a great speaker who was born that way. But because most presentations are generic, boring, or cookie-cutter, when you decide to introduce one new element, you'll quickly set yourself apart. So why not take a risk? You may trip and stumble on occasion, but it's just as likely that you'll soar.

13

YOUR FORMULA FOR SUCCESS: ONE STEP AT A TIME

Learning new techniques is a process. Make sure you've successfully incorporated each skill before moving ahead. Establish working models and put them into play. Presenting well is a long-term commitment, not a race to the finish line.

SOWING THE SEEDS

On those rare occasions when I meet a woman who enjoys public speaking, I'm always curious to hear her story. Sometimes she'll say that she was on her high school or college debate team; other times she'll tell me that she sang in a choir, played an instrument competitively, or performed as a member of an improvisational troupe. The common thread is that, from a very young age, she had experience being onstage. As a result, she understood that rejection and criticism comes with the territory, and that getting feedback—both negative and positive—makes you better the next time.

If you have daughters, nieces, or young women whom you mentor, recommend they engage in an activity that puts them in the public eye—whether it's performing in community theater, working in sales, or taking a volunteer leadership role in a professional organization.

When you put yourself in front of an audience early on, you can hone your communication skills without experiencing the same level of self-judgment that affects many adults. Once you've reduced your fear and anxiety, you can concentrate more on engaging the audience—rather than simply trying to survive the experience.

A few months ago, my grandniece, **Hally**, visited from Oklahoma. She had just turned three and, like most girls her age, was enamored with the Disney movie *Frozen*. We had invited about a dozen friends over for dinner. Hally sat quietly during the adult conversation even though I could tell that she was bored. I was amazed she had the patience. She didn't interrupt the adults or try to be the center of attention.

Afterward, we had congregated outside when Hally decided it was finally her turn. She positioned herself so that everyone could see her and belted out her favorite movie's theme song, "Let It Go," at the top of her lungs. Just in case someone might miss her performance, she skipped in front of us with her arms outstretched, grinning from ear to ear. I marveled at this little girl's complete lack of self-consciousness as well as the pure delight she took in entertaining her audience.

There's no question that performing or leading others is in her future.

But what about the rest of us who dreaded reading our essays in front of the class, never tried out for a play, or always worked behind the scenes?

EMULATE THE BEST

As adults, the road to being out front is tough and difficult, but absolutely achievable. Start by observing speakers you like or respect. What makes them exceptional? Is it the way they enjoy sharing their observations or making eye contact with the audience? Are they laser-focused when delivering their material? Are they comfortable onstage? Can you feel their desire to connect with you?

Watching others provides us with a wealth of insights. Workshop participants often tell me that they changed their content after they watched and listened to the colleagues who preceded them in the training. But as my old film teacher used to say, "We learn more from watching bad movies than watching excellent movies where the technique is invisible and the execution seamless."

Emulating others still requires that we make their techniques our own. To be successful, it's imperative that we remain genuine. And becoming a proficient speaker is an ongoing process, with fits and starts along the way. It's a marathon, not a sprint to the finish line.

Even the most accomplished presenters will sometimes stumble over their words, forget where they were, or say the wrong thing. When any of these missteps occur, just move on. Audiences have short memories. Replaying the mistake in your head will only make it worse. Instead, remember your Intention and recommit to your material. If you sense that you're losing your audience, adjust your material or delivery accordingly: Engage the audience by asking a question, telling a story, or using a low-tech approach to describe your content another way.

If you sense that you're losing your audience, adjust your material or delivery accordingly.

Audiences appreciate someone who is nimble and can smoothly move past a mistake, a heckler, or a client who isn't interested. I've seen it happen more than once. You can transform the harshest critic when you take ownership of your material, exhibit unwavering commitment, or powerfully advocate for your position.

But what happens when you witness a speaker who can't recover, keeps apologizing, or is so flustered that her discomfort sucks all the air out of the room? At first, I feel bad for her and sincerely hope she can reestablish her authority and connection to the material. But if her anxiety continues, my empathy turns to irritation and frustration, because I know it shouldn't be about her.

Remember the acronym WIIFM, or "What's In It For Me?" No one really cares if you stumble, if your blouse is last year's fashion, or you haven't had strong enough coffee. Truly, all we're thinking is, "What can you contribute to our lives, our well-being, or our intellect?"

I've learned that my strength is interacting with the audience rather than lecturing. I'm perfectly comfortable shaping someone's self-introduction or client example. I may not be good at telling a joke, but I have a few one-liners that I like to interject into a presentation, such as this quotation from Napoleon: "Never interrupt your enemy when he's making a mistake."[108]

I enjoy customizing our presentations to a specific audience, so I spend time interviewing attendees before each talk. I never want to be the motivational speaker who in her opening remarks says, "I'm excited to be here in . . ." and then whips her head around to read the banner behind her to see which city she's in or which company she's presenting to.

SEIZE EVERY OPPORTUNITY

For women, one of the biggest obstacles to becoming great speakers is the pressure to always be our best. This standard of excellence is very difficult, if not impossible, to achieve. Even A-list comics try out their material in small clubs before going on television or performing on the big stages. How else can they perfect their timing, listen for the jokes that bomb versus the ones that get a laugh, or exhibit the ease that makes them so enjoyable?

The same holds true for presenters. If you turn down most speaking opportunities, but then suddenly are committed (or forced) to speak, your anxiety intensifies. You haven't built up to it. If you're like most women, you'll focus on the potential for failure, rather than the ingredients for success. Think about it. If you don't try out your material ahead of time, you won't have a baseline for what works or the confidence that you'll do well.

Beth is a forensic certified public accountant who serves as an expert witness in divorce cases. During an Eloqui workshop we asked her to construct and deliver a make-or-break, five-minute presentation.

First, David and I reviewed the critical elements of structure: identifying your Intention and choosing the right Role. Then we gave the participants opening triggers, taught storytelling techniques, made a case for organizing their material into three buckets, and presented seven ways to close.

Beth resisted. The structure seemed overly simplistic to her and didn't reflect her responsibility to educate rather than persuade. We let it be. One week after the workshop, we received the following email.

"Warn your students that once they take your class, opportunities to speak will unexpectedly come their way, and they will feel obligated to say yes or feel like a bit of a fraud. Such is what happened to me this week.

"I got back from taking your immersion workshop on Sunday and had a ton of work to catch up on. On Tuesday I received an email from the managing partner

that I was to speak on Friday at our annual firm meeting in front of 200 partners and employees.

"My initial reaction was that I don't have time. I had to ask myself if I was serious about public speaking or not and if I was, I had to commit to saying yes—not just now but always. On Wednesday I learned I had five minutes, and they needed my slides by 3 P.M. that day.

"I did what any good Analyzer would do and began researching! I pulled out my Eloqui workbook and began with my Intention. I figured out my Opening, prepared my OSB [Obstacle, Solution, Benefit] and my Closing. The information you provided gave me the structure and focus to get to the point (which, as you know, is a little difficult for us Analyzers) and it worked beautifully.

"The managing partner, Steve, is an Accelerator. A few minutes into my speech I looked over at him and realized I still had his attention—so I knew it was going well.

"Afterwards, Steve approached me on three occasions to tell me how well I did and that I made quite an impression. He said he loved the opening, which grabbed his attention and kept it because he wasn't sure where I was going next. I cannot tell you how many people came up to me and said it was the best presentation that day. One employee who has been there for over ten years said it was the best she had ever seen.

"I am new to the firm this year, and what I do is very different from the rest of the company. I had limited time to prepare and I had five minutes to make an impression. The tools, the practice, the ideas, the feedback, and the guidance I received during the workshop allowed me to give a memorable speech with little time to prepare, and opened the door to new working relationships and business. At the party afterward, one of my colleagues approached me with a new client and later that afternoon, I was included in an email for another potential case.

"Thank you so much! My presentation would have been much different without your influence and much less effective."

Beth's comments are gratifying. However, sometimes a client will tell us that she didn't improve after being trained in our techniques. What went wrong? The culprit is usually that the client tried to incorporate every one of the new skills all at once. Beware of this pitfall. When you've spent most of your adult life following one prescription, it's not easy or simple to make a drastic change or unwind old habits.

Many women are overachievers and motivated to succeed, so they study the materials we give them and ask for more homework. I recommend incorporating one new skill at a time, such as telling a story, moving down-stage right to make an important point, or having a creative open that links to your presentation.

Spend time working on the new skill or technique. Feel it out. Does it suit you? How does the audience respond? When this technique has become ingrained and automatic, then you're ready to add another one. As master interviewer Barbara Walters said, "One may walk over the highest mountain one step at a time."[109]

The key is embedding techniques into your muscle memory. You don't want the audience recognizing and identifying you as an Eloqui speaker. You do want the audience to be impressed with your individuality.

Accept any and all speaking invitations. For example, you could introduce yourself at a networking event, give a toast at a party, or speak briefly to an audience of your peers. Choose the setting and audience that will give you the most confidence and create the least amount of anxiety.

DOUBLE YOUR PLEASURE

I'm incredibly fortunate. My partner, David, is a stage actor, corporate spokes-person, and on-camera talent. Before we connected, he was mostly a solo act; now we both prefer delivering keynotes as a team. And according to evaluations and client reviews, we're better together than individually.

There are many advantages to working with a partner. We can engage audiences more effectively because we have different perspectives. While David is talking, I can formulate what I'm going to say next, and vice versa. When he's listening in second chair, he can be thinking of questions to ask me that reflect the audience's perspective and specific needs. We can prompt each other to tell an appropriate story. I know David has my back and that he'll fill in if I forget a concept, word, or name. And David can take the big-picture, Seasoned Veteran perspective, leaving me to be the Facilitator and cover the details or process.

Our duo works just as effectively when we pitch for business. We're frequently asked to train clients in handoff techniques or team presenting, because they've watched us exhibiting these same skills.

Look at your life. Who complements your skills, style, and expertise? Partner with someone who is different from you. Audiences are attracted to variety and different points of view. It doesn't make sense to present with someone who has identical strengths. Are you better with details or the big picture? Are you lively or self-contained? Are you more seasoned or just starting out? Once you have a partner (or partners) you trust, you can focus on what you do best. Since you don't have to learn *their* material, you're saving yourself precious time and effort. And a great partner allows you to play to your strengths.

There are some caveats. It's important to find a partner who has a similar work ethic and attitude toward rehearsing. For example, if you tend to prepare thoroughly, you don't want to team up with someone who waits until the last minute to review her material. I remember the reputation of the great actor Spencer Tracy, who was known to give his best takes the first or second time delivering his lines. It didn't work well when he played opposite an actor in a scene whose performance improved with each take. Tracy would be stale by the time the other actor was hitting his stride.[110]

In our partnership, I'm the organizer. I keep track of where we plan to go next in our presentation and cue David. I don't expect him to lead. Knowing your partner's abilities makes all the difference. But even though we've been living and presenting together for many years, we still get frustrated with each other. So we developed our own signals.

For example, if one of us is speaking too long on a particular topic, the other discreetly gives the "C" sign with one hand: "Shorten up your comments." Of course, your partner needs to look at you to see the sign and then follow it. (Nobody's perfect.) Still, it's better than kicking the other person under the table, tapping her on the arm, or interrupting her in the middle of a sentence.

Here's another guideline we follow. If one of us goes off in a different or unplanned direction, the other must follow. There's no eye-rolling, looking aghast, or saying something to that effect. We keep our reactions to ourselves, and act as if it's all part of our plan (even when it's not).

David has taught me that when you're "on the ice" you're a professional and have a responsibility to the audience (and your reputation) to act like one. This doesn't mean we don't discuss or argue about it afterward, but that's in private. We're often asked how we manage to work together. People will say, "If I had to work with my husband (or wife), we'd kill each other." One key reason for our success is that we do our assessments in private while putting on a positive face in public.

RISK EQUALS REWARD

In my many years of coaching and training executives, I believe what keeps them from achieving greatness is playing it safe. Although this approach is a major impediment to success, it remains the default mode for many women speakers. As I've noted, if you avoid taking risks, you'll fail to set yourself apart. You won't be seen as exhibiting passion or commitment. And you'll probably resort to educating your audience, rather than persuading them. Think about it. No artist, performer, or literary giant plays it safe. You may not always like or agree with what they produce. But by breaking new ground, they inspire and lead instead of following the pack. This is also true in business. I'm not promising that your presentations will always be well received. But you'll have the satisfaction of knowing that your words had integrity, you showed up authentically, and you didn't hide behind the veneer of being safe.

> In my many years of coaching and training executives, I believe what keeps them from achieving greatness is playing it safe.

There's no doubt that taking risks will catapult you into the realm of exceptional speakers. If this is also your goal, make the commitment. Be out front. There has never been a better time for women to take the lead and let nothing stand in our way. Seize the moment, so you'll never have to say, "If only . . ."

ACKNOWLEDGMENTS

Thank you to the women who took the time and effort to pay attention to a blue-collar kid from the south side of Chicago. Ada Deer, Nancy Lurie, and Dr. Lonnie Barbach—you gave me encouragement, wisdom, and a window into what it takes to be a person of influence. The best way I can honor you is to pass on what I've learned to others.

To the hundreds of female clients we have trained, coached, and mentored—every time I see you succeed, I'm thrilled. You make me better at what I do. You give my life purpose, and reinforce that this is what I was meant to do.

To my close circle of confidants, who read various drafts of this manuscript and whose input I value: Natasha Billawala (researcher and initial editor); Larissa Berringer and Eden Gillott Bowe (providing their youthful perspective); Dr. Lonnie Barbach (for a lifetime of coaching); Carla Hatley (insights from a seasoned performer); Marc Hankin (Eloqui's most fervent supporter); Jonathan Fitzgarrald (marketing genius); Merrily Pierson (whom I've loved since film school); Barbara Henricks (for her public relations and media perspective); Karen Cates (an outstanding professor, who printed the manuscript and meticulously noted suggested changes); and Sally Phillips (who coaches and understands women executives). I can't thank you enough.

I'm most grateful for my partner, David, who has given me many gifts—not the least of which are the weeks he's devoted to supporting me during the writing and revising of this book.

Together, David and I translate performance techniques for business professionals. Even though he spent his entire prior career as a solo performer, David graciously shares the stage whenever we speak and train. He patiently taught me to fight my fears so that I could be a powerful force in other women's lives. Now I look forward to each new project and the opportunity to give women the skills and courage to become fearless speakers. Because of David, I'm becoming the best expression of me. There's no greater gift.

APPENDIX: TRUSTED ADVISOR TEMPLATE©

To establish trust and engineer the perception that you are a Trusted Advisor, we recommend the following. Although this order is effective, there are no hard-and-fast rules.

1. **EMPATHY:** Caring is the critical first step to establishing trust. Begin with a version of "It must be difficult to . . ." and wait for the other party to respond. Express authentic concern.
2. **UNDERSTANDING:** Back up empathy with direct knowledge of a potential client's industry or specific business. Make assumptions based on your other clients in that industry.
3. **ASK GOOD QUESTIONS:** Further develop trust by asking targeted questions, seeking details. Retain these details to note in the conversation. Also, listen without directing the conversation back to you. Better to go deep than wide.
4. **INCLUDE LONG-TERM ASSOCIATIONS:** Trusted Advisors keep clients for years. It is essential to sprinkle in references to other long-held client relationships.
5. **DIRECT RECOMMENDATION OR CLIENT ANECDOTE:** Make a judgment call on whether to offer a direct advisement. If you feel it is too soon, deliver a client anecdote, matched to the prospective client's situation and challenges.

LANGUAGE AND BEHAVIOR:

Warm, confident, direct, and collaborative. Unlike a Motivator, a Trusted Advisor is patient and low-key, with a collegial demeanor that draws people in.

GLOSSARY

Accelerator: One of the four communication types from the Eloqui Communication Index. Accelerators are bottom-line oriented, charismatic, competitive, and impatient. They are often CEOs, business leaders, or entrepreneurs.

Analyzer: One of the four communication types from the Eloqui Communication Index. Analyzers are thoughtful individuals who enjoy research and delving into details. To be convinced, Analyzers require context and hard evidence, as well as an understanding of how a project or idea fits into the overall system. They are often scientists, engineers, analysts, and attorneys.

Anecdote: A short account or narrative of an event that's brief, engaging, and relevant. Not to be confused with "antidote."

Attention precedes comprehension: The necessity of firing up the attentional area of the brain to ensure an audience grasps the concept.

Bookend: A device used in closing, whereby the speaker uses a variation on the opening or references it to complete the presentation.

Bridging: A term that describes how to prepare immediately before speaking. Elements of bridging include clearing your mind and transitioning from your everyday self to the selected Role while keeping your Intention in focus.

Collaborator: One of the four communication types from the Eloqui Communication Index. Collaborators have a high level of emotional intelligence and value contribution. They gravitate to human interactions, and choose fields like human resources and the nonprofit sector, where they can make the greatest difference.

Cueing: Signaling a partner or team member to speak by using a downward vocal inflection and putting a period on the end of a sentence or phrase.

Diaphragmatic breathing: Also called "belly breathing." Taking air into the lower abdomen to create breath support for longer sentences or sections of text.

Downstage: Moving toward the audience.

Downward inflection: A vocal "period" that indicates you've concluded a thought or statement. Also, an audio cue to signal your partner to enter the conversation.

Eloqui Communication Index: Based on demeanor and the way people speak. Eloqui has observed that specific demeanors are reflected in four categories: Accelerator, Pragmatist, Collaborator, and Analyzer. The purpose of the ECI is to determine someone's communication style and then mirror her style to be more effective or persuasive.

Encoding specificity: Matching, as closely as possible, the rehearsal environment to the actual space where the presentation will be delivered—for the purpose of making the presenter more comfortable and embedding the talk into memory.

Engineer perception: Termed "impression management" in social psychology, this concept allows the speaker to create the manner in which he or she is viewed by the audience.

Flow: A state of total immersion in a task, free of distraction.

Fourth wall: The imagined barrier between speaker and audience. Crossing downstage toward the audience, asking questions, or interacting with audience members are effective methods for "breaking through the fourth wall."

Framing: Using a visual image, simile, or metaphor at the beginning of a presentation to create audience reference points for the material that follows.

Glossophobia: Stage fright, or the fear of being discovered as a fake. Traditional public speaking provokes anxiety or glossophobia in approximately 75 percent of the general population.

Handoff: Passing the baton in group presenting; completing a thought and signaling your partner to pick up the cue.

Impression management: A process to influence perceptions people have by regulating and controlling information in social interactions or speaking.

Information overload: Exceeding the amount of information that can be retained by the listener.

Intention: Synonymous with objective or goal. A precise, active statement best not stated aloud that sums up the primary desire of the speaker; for example, "I'll prove that our services are critical to your success."

Lavaliere: A small microphone clipped to one's lapel, shirt, tie, or blouse.

Leave-behind deck: A full, text-rich printed version of a PowerPoint presentation. To be left with the client or audience, so the presenter can use a leaner, more visual version for her talk.

Marking: Rehearsal technique. Walking through the movement and content of a talk without full energy or using the exact words. Method to encode a talk into memory. *See also* Stumble through.

Mnemonic: A memory device that aids the retention of rote information. For example, My Very Educated Mother Just Served Us Nine Pizzas is a mnemonic for remembering the names of the planets in the solar system plus Pluto in their order of distance from the sun: Mercury, Venus, Earth, Mars, Jupiter, Saturn, Uranus, Neptune, and Pluto.

Mood congruence: A memory process that selectively retrieves memories that match or are consistent with one's current mood. For speakers, it is critical to attain a state of readiness and confidence so that past memories of the same state are brought to mind.

Multi-tasking: Being able to perform several tasks simultaneously. Evidence shows that this can only be done when one or more of the tasks are learned to a level of automaticity.

Obstacle, solution, and benefit (OSB): An Eloqui template and rhetorical device for the three key components in telling a story or anecdote.

On the ice: Theatrical term meaning onstage in front of an audience.

Potted up: Audio term, indicating an increase in volume.

Power of three: The cardinal number for memory retention. Units of threes are found in religions, nursery rhymes, and sports. For speakers, this is the perfect number for lists, sections, or "buckets" in the main part of a speech.

Pragmatist: One of the four communication types from the Eloqui Communication Index. Pragmatists are organized, goal-oriented individuals who appreciate value as well as accountability from others. They are the prototypical stage manager and gravitate toward positions where there is a specific outcome, like COO, manager, or division leader.

Presenter deck: The PowerPoint version that the presenter uses; this version has teaser titles, is visual, and includes only salient details. *See also* Leave-behind deck.

Priming: Activating left- or right-brain functions. Analysis or listing data primes the left brain, serial thinking, debate, and argument. Story, emotion, or shared values prime the right brain to facilitate decision making and buy-in.

Putting a button on it: Emphasizing the last word of a sentence.

Role: Device for driving Intention; the speaking filter. The choice of Role facilitates impression management through congruence of behavior and speech.

Second chair: A member of a team who is not speaking at any given time during the presentation. Person in second chair engineers assent by actively listening to and agreeing with the speaker, or first chair.

Self-monitoring: Observing, evaluating, and regulating performance while one is presenting. Deadly for speakers, it interferes with presenting and most types of performance because it splits attention.

Sense memory: A technique that involves recalling an experience (i.e., utilizing sight, sound, smell, taste, and touch) to evoke a specific state that the speaker wishes to exhibit.

Simile: A figure of speech in which two distinct things are compared using "like" or "as," as in "like a knife through butter" or "as wholesome as apple pie."

Stumble through: Rehearsal technique. Going through the motions and words of a presentation, without full energy, as a means of keeping a talk fresh in memory. *See also* Marking.

Take: Film term for each time a scene is recorded, as in "take two."

Telegraph: A signal that a speaker is about to move, which can be indicated by a physical gesture or looking to the intended direction of travel.

Tells: Physical signals from a speaker that indicate what they are about to do, like raising the toes and ball of one foot (or balancing on the heel) to signify an upcoming move or leaning in the direction one is about to move. Speakers are rarely aware of "tells."

Upstage: Away from the audience toward the rear of the stage. The slang term "upstaging" means moving toward the back of the space, causing the other performer or presenter to turn his back to the audience. A PowerPoint screen can also upstage a speaker.

Visual snapshot: A highly compressed image, delivered by a speaker, that expands in the imagination of the listener because of the visual details embedded in it.

ENDNOTES

Introduction

1. National Institute of Public Health, "Fear of Public Speaking Statistics," Statistic Brain Research Institute, November 23, 2013, accessed February 26, 2016, http://www.statisticbrain.com/fear-of-public-speaking-statistics

Chapter One—Inspirational and Powerful Female Icons

2. Lea Carpenter, "Lesson 21: Gloria Steinem's Aphorisms; Fish, Power, Love, Bunnies, and Life," *Big Think*, 2012, accessed February 26, 2016, http://bigthink.com/english-lessons/lesson-21-gloria-steinems-aphorisms-fish-power-love-bunnies-and-life
3. Laura Miller, "Brilliant Careers: Germaine Greer," *Salon*, June 22, 1999, accessed February 26, 2016, https://people.kth.se/~gunnarj/AAPORTFn/PRL/greer-miller1.html
4. Erica Jong, "*Fear of Dying: A Novel*," Macmillan Publishers, accessed February 26, 2016, http://us.macmillan.com/fearofdying/ericajong
5. "American Rhetoric: Top 100 Speeches of All Time," *American Rhetoric* (undated), accessed February 26, 2016, http://www.americanrhetoric.com/top100speechesall.html
6. Barbara Charline Jordan, "1976 Democratic National Convention Keynote Address," *American Rhetoric*, delivered July 12, 1976, accessed March 8, 2016, http://www.americanrhetoric.com/speeches/barbarajordan1976dnc.html
7. Jone Johnson, "Bella Abzug Quotes," About.com, last modified August 26, 2015, accessed February 26, 2016, http://womenshistory.about.com/cs/quotes/a/qu_bella_abzug.htm
8. "Bella Abzug Quotes," *BrainyQuote* (unattributed and undated), accessed February 26, 2016, http://www.brainyquote.com/quotes/authors/b/bella_abzug.html#qLzRdhCUivzggw2M
9. "Schroeder, Patricia Scott," History, Art & Archives (unattributed and undated), US House of Representatives, accessed February 26, 2016, http://history.house.gov/People/detail/21313

10. "Patricia Schroeder Quotes," *BrainyQuote* (unattributed and undated), accessed February 26, 2016, http://www.brainyquote.com/quotes/authors/p/patricia_schroeder.html#Gh7A6P M6QZT5Gwi3.9

11. Ibid.

12. "Ada E. Deer Facts," *Encyclopedia of World Biography* (unattributed and undated), accessed February 26, 2016, http://biography.yourdictionary.com/ada-e-deer#Q4P0IkwWYYUgSEfQ99

13. Ibid.

14. Ibid.

15. Jone Johnson, "Bella Abzug Quotes," About.com, last modified August 26, 2015, accessed February 26, 2016, http://womenshistory.about.com/cs/quotes/a/qu_bella_abzug.htm

16. Ibid.

17. "Biography of Susan B. Anthony," Susan B. Anthony House (unattributed and undated), accessed February 26, 2016, https://susanbanthonyhouse.org/her-story/biography.php

18. Brian MacQuarrie, "Malala Yousafzai Addresses Harvard Audience," *Boston Globe*, September 28, 2013, accessed February 26, 2016, http://www.bostonglobe.com/metro/2013/09/27/ malala-yousafzai-pakistani-teen-shot-taliban-tells-harvard-audience-that-education-right-for-all /6cZBan0M4J3cAnmRZLfUmI/story.html

19. Victoria L. Brescoll, "Who Takes the Floor and Why: Gender, Power, and Volubility in Organizations," *Administrative Science Quarterly*, December 2011, 56.4, 622–641, accessed March 8, 2016, http://asq.sagepub.com/content/56/4/622.short#cited-by

20. Sebastian Dillon, "What Happens When Women Are Asked to Speak Up during Business Meetings," *Nextshark*, January 12, 2015, accessed February 26, 2016, http://nextshark.com/ what-happens-when-women-are-asked-to-speak-up-during-business-meetings

21. Ibid.

22. Anita Woolley, Thomas W. Malone, and Christopher F. Chabris, "Why Some Teams Are Smarter Than Others," Sunday Review, *New York Times*, January 16, 2015, accessed February 26, 2016, http://www.nytimes.com/2015/01/18/opinion/sunday/why-some-teams-are-smarter-than-others.html

23. Sheryl Sandberg and Adam Grant, "Speaking While Female: Sheryl Sandberg and Adam Grant on Why Women Stay Quiet at Work," Sunday Review, *New York Times*, January 12, 2015, accessed March 8, 2016, http://www.nytimes.com/2015/01/11/opinion/sunday/speaking -while-female.html

24. Ibid.

25. *Rolling Stone* staff, "Watch Samantha Bee Tear Down Kansas Senator on 'Full Frontal' Premiere," *Rolling Stone*, February 9, 2016, accessed March 8, 2016, http://www.rollingstone.com/ tv/news/watch-samantha-bee-tear-down-kansas-senator-on-full-frontal-premiere-20160209

26. Ana Marie Cox, "Samantha Bee Likes to Make Things Uncomfortable," Talk section, *New York Times Magazine*, February 8, 2016, accessed February 26, 2016, http://www.nytimes.com/2016 /02/14/magazine/samantha-bee-likes-to-make-things-uncomfortable.html

27. Jill Bolte Taylor, "My Stroke of Insight," TED Talks, filmed February 2008, accessed February 26, 2016, http://www.ted.com/talks/jill_bolte_taylor_s_powerful_stroke_of_insight

28. Brené Brown, "The Power of Vulnerability," TED Talks, filmed June 2010, accessed February 26, 2016, https://www.ted.com/talks/brene_brown_on_vulnerability?language=en://www .bing.com/videos

29. John Horn, Nicole Sperling, and Doug Smith, "Unmasking Oscar: Academy Voters Overwhelmingly White, Male," *Los Angeles Times*, February 19, 2012, accessed March 8, 2016, http://www.latimes.com/entertainment/movies/academy/la-et-unmasking-oscar-academy -project-20120219-story.html

30. Colleen Leahey, Caroline Fairchild, and Valentina Zarya, "Women CEOs in the Fortune 500," *Fortune*, last updated December 21, 2015, accessed March 8, 2016, http://fortune.com/2013 /05/09/women-ceos-in-the-fortune-500

31. Sheryl Sandberg and Adam Grant, "Speaking While Female: Sheryl Sandberg and Adam Grant on Why Women Stay Quiet at Work," Sunday Review, *New York Times*, January 12, 2015, accessed March 8, 2016, http://www.nytimes.com/2015/01/11/opinion/sunday/speaking -while-female.html

32. Gregory Ferenstein, "Why Women Now Outnumber Men at the Top US Video-Game Design School," *ReadWrite*, January 22, 2016, accessed March 8, 2016, http://readwrite.com/2016/01 /22/video-game-women-usc-gender-parity

Chapter Two—Exorcise the Demons: Dispelling Myths about Public Speaking

33. Erik Deckers, "What Malcolm Gladwell REALLY Said about the 10,000 Hour Rule," *Pro Blog Service* (blog), March 15, 2012, accessed March 8, 2016, http://problogservice.com/2012/03/ 15/what-malcolm-gladwell-really-said-about-the-10000-hour-rule

34. Shivananda R. Koteshwar, "Book Summary: *Blink: The Power of Thinking Without Thinking*," *SlideShare*, November 16, 2013, accessed March 8, 2016, http://www.slideshare.net/shivoo .koteshwar/book-summary-shivoo6blink

35. *Psychology Today* staff, "What Is Priming?" *Psychology Today* (undated), accessed March 8, 2016, https://www.psychologytoday.com/basics/priming

36. Mark R. Leary, *Self-Presentation: Impression Management and Interpersonal Behavior* (Boulder, CO: Westview Press, 1996).

37. Ibid.

38. Lorne Manly, "Being Careful Out There? Hardly. Steven Bochco and Others on Creating 'Hill Street Blues,'" *New York Times*, May 1, 2014, accessed March 8, 2016, http://www.nytimes .com/2014/05/04/arts/television/steven-bochco-and-others-on-creating-hill-street-blues.html

39. Dave McNary, "Women, Minorities Still Underrepresented as First-Time Episodic TV Directors: DGA Report," *Variety*, September 10, 2015, accessed March 8, 2016, http://variety.com /2015/tv/news/women-minority-directors-tv-dga-first-time-1201590038

40. David Robb, "DGA: Women Directed Only 6.4% of Feature Films in 2013 & 2014," *Deadline. com*, December 9, 2015, accessed March 8, 2016, http://deadline.com/2015/12/dga-report -women-directors-feature-films-female-1201662675

41.   Matthew Weaver, "Kathryn Bigelow Makes History as First Woman to Win Best Director Oscar," *The Guardian*, March 8, 2010, accessed March 8, 2016, http://www.theguardian.com/film/2010/mar/08/kathryn-bigelow-oscars-best-director

42.   "Carrie (2013)," *The Numbers: Where Data and the Movie Business Meet*, Nash Information Services LLC, accessed March 9, 2016, http://www.the-numbers.com/movie/Carrie-(2013)#tab=summary

43.   Tre'vell Anderson, " 'Selma' Director Ava DuVernay on the Secrets to Indie Film Success," *Los Angeles Times*, February 4, 2015, accessed March 8, 2016, http://www.latimes.com/entertainment/movies/moviesnow/la-et-mn-ava-duvernay-film-independent-20150204-story.html

44.   Ibid.

45.   "Ursula Burns Quotes," *BrainyQuote*, accessed February 26, 2016, http://www.brainyquote.com/quotes/authors/u/ursula_burns.html#1ZY1XAW5ky4kCE11.99

46.   Ella L. J. Edmondson Bell, "Ursula Burns: Managing with Heart and Some Soul," *Huffington Post*, last modified November 17, 2011, accessed February 26, 2016, http://www.huffingtonpost.com/ella-l-j-edmondson-bell-phd/ursula-burns-managing-wit_b_498944.html

47.   Margie Warrell, "Glass Ceiling or Glass Cage? Breaking Through the Biggest Barrier Holding Women Back," *Forbes*, August 4, 2013, accessed February 26, 2016, http://www.forbes.com/sites/margiewarrell/2013/08/04/glass-ceiling-or-glass-cage-breaking-through-the-biggest-barrier-holding-women-back

48.   Ryan Gajewski, "Emmys: 'Inside Amy Schumer' Wins Outstanding Variety Sketch Series," *Hollywood Reporter*, September 20, 2015, accessed February 26, 2016, http://www.hollywoodreporter.com/news/inside-amy-schumer-wins-emmy-821009

49.   Sam Stein and Jason Cherkis, "Wendy Davis Opens Up on the Burden of Running as a Feminist Icon in Texas," *Huffington Post*, February 1, 2016, accessed February 26, 2016, http://www.huffingtonpost.com/entry/wendy-davis texas_us_56ae4fa3e4b077d4fe8e7f1e

50.   Allida Black, "Hillary Rodham Clinton," *The First Ladies of the United States of America*, 2009, White House Historical Association, accessed February 26, 2016, https://www.whitehouse.gov/1600/first-ladies/hillaryclinton

51.   "Biography: Hillary Rodham Clinton," *American Experience* (show website), PBS, accessed February 26, 2016, http://www.pbs.org/wgbh/americanexperience/features/biography/clinton-hillary

52.   "Hillary Clinton Fast Facts," *Library* (blog), CNN, last modified January 28, 2016, accessed February 26, 2016, http://www.cnn.com/2012/12/20/us/hillary-clinton---fast-facts/index.html

53.   Ibid.

54.   Aaron Blake, "Hillary Clinton: The 'Most Admired Woman' in the World," *The Fix* (blog), *Washington Post*, December 31, 2012, accessed February 26, 2016, http://www.washingtonpost.com/blogs/the-fix/wp/2012/12/31/hillary-clinton-the-most-admired-woman-in-the-world

55.   Alison Walsh, "Women in the Legal Profession: Improving the Statistics—A Review of the 'Women in the Legal Profession Summit' Recordings," June 25, 2008, HB Litigation Conferences, accessed April 4, 2016, http://litigationconferences.com/women-in-the-legal-profession-improving-the-statistics

56.   Deborah Chang and Sonia Chopra, "Where Are All the Women Lawyers? Diversity in the Legal Profession in California: 2015," *FORUM*, Consumer Attorneys of California, September/

October 2015, accessed February 26, 2016, http://www.njp.com/wp-content/uploads/article/article36.pdf

57. Marlisse Silver Sweeney, "The Female Lawyer Exodus," *Litmus Test* (blog), The Daily Beast, July 31, 2013, accessed February 26, 2016, http://www.thedailybeast.com/witw/articles/2013/07/31/the-exodus-of-female-lawyers.html

58. "BLS Spotlight on Statistics: The Recession of 2007–2009," US Department of Labor, February 2012, accessed February 26, 2016, http://www.bls.gov/spotlight/2012/recession/audio.htm

Chapter Three—Afraid to Misspeak: Perfection Is a Bitch

59. The Impostor Syndrome, sometimes called impostor phenomenon or fraud syndrome, is a psychological phenomenon in which people are unable to internalize their accomplishments. Despite external evidence of their competence, those with the syndrome remain convinced that they are frauds and do not deserve the success they have achieved. Proof of success is dismissed as luck, timing, or a result of deceiving others into thinking they are more intelligent and competent than they believe themselves to be.

60. Robert Ardrey, *The Social Contract: A Personal Inquiry into the Evolutionary Sources of Order and Disorder* (Oxford: StoryDesign Ltd., 2014).

61. Matt Sloane, Jason Hanna, and Dana Ford, "'Never, Ever Give Up:' Diana Nyad Completes Historic Cuba-to-Florida Swim," CNN, September 3, 2013, accessed February 26, 2016, http://www.cnn.com/2013/09/02/world/americas/diana-nyad-cuba-florida-swim

62. Jennifer Kay, "Diana Nyad's Skeptics Question Integrity of Swim, Use of Mask, Possible Assistance by Boat," Associated Press, last modified November 8, 2013, accessed February 26, 2016, http://www.huffingtonpost.com/2013/09/08/diana-nyad-swim-rules-boat-mask_n_3890216.html

63. Motivation.com, accessed February 26, 2016, http://www.motivation.com/quotes/1152

Chapter Four—What Sets Us Apart: Playing to Our Strengths

64. Gord Hotchkiss, "Human Hardware: Men and Women," *Just Behave* (blog), *Search Engine Land*, April 18, 2008, accessed February 26, 2016, http://searchengineland.com/human-hardware-men-and-women-13614

65. Elizabeth Palermo, "Women May Be Better Than Men . . . at Multitasking," *LiveScience*, October 28, 2013, accessed February 26, 2016, http://www.livescience.com/40740-women-better-at-multitasking.html

66. Ibid.

67. Gord Hotchkiss, "Human Hardware: Men and Women," *Just Behave* (blog), *Search Engine Land*, April 18, 2008, accessed February 26, 2016, http://searchengineland.com/human-hardware-men-and-women-13614

68. "Normal Testosterone and Estrogen Levels in Women," *WebMD*, reviewed by Melinda Ratini, DO, MS, November 21, 2014, accessed March 10, 2016, http://www.webmd.com/women/guide/normal-testosterone-and-estrogen-levels-in-women

69. Jerett Rion, "Male Testosterone Levels Increase when Victorious in Competition against Rivals, but Not Friends, MU Researchers Find," MU News Bureau, University of Missouri, May 14, 2013, accessed February 26, 2016, http://munews.missouri.edu/news-releases/2013/0514-male-testosterone-levels-increase-when-victorious-in-competition-against-rivals-but-not-friends-mu-researchers-find

70. Christopher Bergland, "Testosterone Fuels Both Competition and Protectiveness," *The Athlete's Way* (blog), *Psychology Today*, October 3, 2013, accessed February 26, 2016, https://www.psychologytoday.com/blog/the-athletes-way/201310/testosterone-fuels-both-competition-and-protectiveness

71. "Male and Female Voices Affect Brain Differently," University of Sheffield, News Department, July 12, 2005, accessed March 10, 2016, https://www.sheffield.ac.uk/news/nr/422-1.174743

72. David Walsh, "Boys' and Girls' Brains: What's the Difference?" Expert Q&A, PBS.org, September 2012, accessed March 10, 2016, http://www.pbs.org/parents/experts/archive/2012/09/boy-and-girl-brains-whats-the.html

73. Society for Neuroscience, "Language Protein Differs in Males, Females," *ScienceDaily*, February 19, 2013, accessed March 10, 2016, www.sciencedaily.com/releases/2013/02/130219172153.htm

74. University of California, Irvine, "Intelligence in Men and Women Is a Gray and White Matter," *ScienceDaily*, January 22, 2005, accessed March 10, 2016, www.sciencedaily.com/releases/2005/01/050121100142.htm

75. Michael Rothman, "5 Things Sandra Bullock Learned while Googling Herself," *Good Morning America*, January 6, 2014, accessed February 26, 2016, http://abcnews.go.com/blogs/entertainment/2014/01/5-things-sandra-bullock-learned-while-googling-herself

76. IMDb entry for *A League of Their Own*, The Internet Movie Database website (undated), accessed February 26, 2016, http://www.imdb.com/title/tt0104694/quotes

77. Janice Im, Rebecca Parlakian, and Carol A. Osborn, "Stories: Their Powerful Role in Early Language and Literacy," *Beyond the Journal: Young Children on the Web*, January 2007, accessed February 26, 2016, https://www.naeyc.org/files/yc/file/200701/BTJRocknroll.pdf

78. Ibid.

79. Ibid.

80. Frank Rose, "The Art of Immersion: Why Do We Tell Stories?" *Wired*, March 8, 2011, accessed March 4, 2016, http://www.wired.com/2011/03/why-do-we-tell-stories/all

81. Deborah Fallows, "How Women and Men Use the Internet," Pew Research Center report, December 28, 2005, accessed March 4, 2016, http://www.pewinternet.org/2005/12/28/how-women-and-men-use-the-internet

82. Robert Frager, Ph.D., and James Fadiman, Ph.D., "Transpersonal Pioneers: Carl Jung," in *Personality and Personal Growth*, 6th ed. (New York: Pearson, 2005), 56. Excerpt accessed March 4, 2016, http://www.sofia.edu/about/history/transpersonal-pioneers-carl-jung

83. Frank Rose, "The Art of Immersion: Why Do We Tell Stories?," *Wired*, March 8, 2011, accessed March 4, 2016, http://www.wired.com/2011/03/why-do-we-tell-stories/all

84. Maya Angelou, "Inaugural Poem," January 20, 1993, *EServer.org*, accessed March 10, 2016, http://poetry.eserver.org/angelou.html

85. Peter Guber, *Tell to Win: Connect, Persuade, and Triumph with the Hidden Power of Story* (New York: Crown Business, 2011).

86. Jonathan Gottschall, *The Storytelling Animal: How Stories Make Us Human* (New York: Mariner Books, 2013).

87. Jonathan Gottschall, "Why Storytelling Is the Ultimate Weapon," *Co.Create* (blog), *Fast Company*, May 2, 2012, accessed March 4, 2016, http://www.fastcocreate.com/1680581/why-storytelling -is-the-ultimate-weapon

88. Dennis Nishi, "To Persuade People, Tell Them a Story: Narrative Is a Powerful Way to Get a Message Across," *Wall Street Journal*, November 9, 2013, accessed March 4, 2016, http://www .wsj.com/articles/SB10001424052702303482504579177651982683162

89. Michael J. Newman, "The Importance of Storytelling as a Tool in the Practice of Law," *The Legal Intelligencer*, April 19, 2013, accessed March 4, 2016, http://www.thelegalintelligencer .com/id=1202596665020/The-Importance-of-Storytelling-as-a-Tool-in-the-Practice-of -Law?slreturn=20150118180200

Chapter Six—The Value of Using Strong Technique

90. Jacques Steinberg, "Don Hewitt, Creator of '60 Minutes,' Dies at 86," *New York Times*, August 19, 2009, http://www.nytimes.com/2009/08/20/business/media/20hewitt.html

Chapter Seven—Engage the Audience from Start to Finish

91. The White House, "President Obama Speaks at 9/11 Museum Dedication," US Government, posted May 15, 2014, accessed March 4, 2016, http://www.whitehouse.gov/photos-and-video/ video/2014/05/15/president-obama-speaks-911-museum-dedication

92. James L. Mason, "Biography of Edmund Gwenn," The Internet Movie Database website, undated, accessed March 4, 2016, http://www.imdb.com/name/nm0350324/bio

Chapter Ten—Serve and Volley: Communication as a Contact Sport

93. "No Battle Plan Survives Contact with the Enemy," post on Lexician website (unattributed), November 1, 2010, accessed March 4, 2016, http://www.lexician.com/lexblog/2010/11/no- battle-plan-survives-contact-with-the-enemy

94. Robert Lane Greene, "George Orwell on Writing: Those Six Little Rules," *Johnson* (column), *The Economist*, July 29, 2013, accessed March 4, 2016, http://www.economist.com/blogs/prospero /2013/07/george-orwell-writing?fsrc=scn/fb/te/bl/ed/georgeorwellonwritingthosesixlittlerules

95. Robert Cialdini, *Influence: The Psychology of Persuasion* (New York: Harper Business, 2006), PDF version accessed March 4, 2016, http://www.academia.edu/7935117/Influence_Psychology _of_Persuasion_by_Robert_Caldini

96. Ibid.

97.   Tim Dahlberg, "Phelps Proves Human After All," Associated Press, July 28, 2012, accessed
       March 4, 2016, http://www.nbcmiami.com/news/sports/NATL-Phelps-Proves-Human-After-
       All--164147056.html

98.   Carolyn Thomas, "Why Doctors Get Sued," *The Ethical Nag*, October 15, 2010, accessed
       March 4, 2016, http://ethicalnag.org/2010/10/15/why-doctors-get-sued

Chapter Twelve—Manage Anxiety and Deliver like a Pro

99.   Sheila Marikar, "Shirley MacLaine Reveals Racy Past," ABC News, April 12, 2011, accessed
       March 4, 2016, http://abcnews.go.com/Entertainment/shirley-maclaine-reveals-racy-past-
       oprah-winfrey/story?id=13355390

100.   Editors of *Encyclopædia Britannica*, "Stanislavsky System: Acting," *Encyclopædia Britannica*, updated
       October 15, 2014, accessed March 7, 2016, http://www.britannica.com/art/Stanislavsky-system

101.   Ibid.

102.   Edward Wisniewski, "Mood Congruent Recall," *International Encyclopedia of the Social Sciences*,
       2008, accessed March 7, 2016, http://www.encyclopedia.com/doc/1G2-3045301621.html

103.   Sharon Waxman, "The Oscar Acceptance Speech: By and Large, It's a Lost Art," *Washington
       Post*, March 21, 1999, accessed March 7, 2016, http://www.washingtonpost.com/wp-srv/style/
       movies/oscars/speeches.htm

104.   Philip A. Higham, "Strong Cues Are Not Necessarily Weak: Thomson and Tulving (1970) and
       The Encoding Specificity Principle Revisited," *Memory & Cognition* 30, no. 1 (January 2002):
       67–80, accessed March 7, 2016, https://www.researchgate.net/publication/11409685_Strong
       _cues_are_not_necessarily_weak_Thomson_and_Tulving_1970_and_the_encoding_specificity
       _principle_revisited

105.   Kevin Hechtkopf, "Rick Perry Fails to Remember What Agency He'd Get Rid of in GOP De-
       bate," CBS News, updated November 10, 2011, accessed March 7, 2016, http://www.cbsnews
       .com/news/rick-perry-fails-to-remember-what-agency-hed-get-rid-of-in-gop-debate

106.   Ibid.

107.   Sandy Schussel, "Beating the 'BUT' Monster," Sandy Schussel website, September 25, 2013,
       accessed March 7, 2016, https://sandyschussel.com/beating-the-but-monster

Chapter Thirteen—Your Formula for Success: One Step at a Time

108.   Michael Moncur, "Quotation 26960," *Michael Moncur's (Cynical) Quotations* (collection), *The
       Quotations Page*, accessed March 7, 2016, http://www.quotationspage.com/quote/26960.html

109.   "Barbara Walters Quotes," *BrainyQuote* (unattributed and undated), accessed April 11, 2016,
       http://www.brainyquote.com/quotes/quotes/b/barbarawal119104.html

110.   "Spencer Tracy Biography," Reality TV World (undated and unattributed), accessed March 7,
       2016, http://www.realitytvworld.com/pophollywood/spencer-tracy/biography

ABOUT THE AUTHOR

Before she co-founded Eloqui with David Booth, Deborah Shames was an award-winning film and television director. She founded the only female-owned production company in the San Francisco Bay Area, Focal Point Productions, which she ran for fifteen years. At Focal Point, Deborah directed luminaries including Wendie Malick, Rita Moreno, Danny Glover, and Angela Lansbury.

Now Deborah coaches executives to enhance their presentation and communication skills. She is frequently engaged as a keynote speaker at national meetings and off-site retreats, conferences, and summits. Her most requested topics include storytelling, team presenting, networking, and business development.

Her company, Eloqui, trains teams to effectively communicate their message. Clients include TD Ameritrade, Amgen, Mattel, Samsung Chemical, and Hyundai Hata, as well as law, financial, and insurance firms. Eloqui partners with clients to identify their strengths and lift them to leadership in their industry.

Eloqui also serves nonprofits, especially for fundraising. From the Pancreatic Cancer Action Network and the Arthritis Foundation to Ability First, they train everyone from the CEO and senior management team to the board members and volunteers.

For ten years, Deborah has led a prominent business development group in Calabasas, California. She was awarded "Consultant of the Year" by the *San Fernando Valley Business Journal*.

Deborah and her partner, David, wrote *Own the Room: Business Presentations That Persuade, Engage & Get Results*. Published by McGraw-Hill, the book is now in its third printing and is a business bestseller.

Be a part of the movement at www.outfront.biz or join the conversation in the Women Out Front group on LinkedIn. Deborah can be reached at info@outfront.biz. Contact Eloqui at 818-225-7991 or visit their website at www.eloqui.biz.

For more Eloqui techniques, check out Own the Room: Business Presentations that Persuade, Engage and Get Results, written by Deborah Shames and David Booth. The book was published by McGraw-Hill in 2010 and has become a business bestseller. Order copies on Amazon: http://tinyurl.com/z50g8jb

It Pays to Speak Well

Eloqui training blends art and science. Every program is customized for each individual or team. Trainers identify your strengths and provide specific tools to be effective in any venue, whether one-on-one in a client meeting, pitching for new business, raising money for your non-profit, or speaking on your area of expertise to your target audience.

Eloqui presentation and communication services include:

- Own the Room corporate workshops
- Keynote speaking by Deborah and David at retreats & conferences
- Individual coaching with the Power of Five program
- Business Development Workshops in Calabasas, California
- Communication Immersion workshops in Santa Fe, New Mexico

Eloqui clients range from new hires to seasoned executives, startups to established firms and Fortune 500 companies. These include Mattel, OneAmerica, Samsung, Hyundai, Wells Fargo, and TD Ameritrade. We've partnered with and supported thousands of business professionals, from sales people and engineers to CEOs, attorneys, CPAs and financial advisors. You too can gain confidence and speak persuasively with impact and style.

Sign up for the Eloqui Tip of the Week or learn more at www.eloqui.biz

tion this ad for a 10% reduced fee on any Eloqui program!

1-818-225-7991